house beautiful

Entertaining

house beautiful

Entertaining

THE EDITORS OF HOUSE BEAUTIFUL MAGAZINE

LOUIS OLIVER GROPP
Editor in Chief

MARGARET KENNEDY
Editor

JANE ELLIS
Food and Entertaining Editor

HEARST BOOKS

NEW YORK

It is the policy of William Morrow and Company, Inc., and its imprints and affiliates, recognizing the importance of preserving what has been written, to print the books we publish on acid-free paper, and we exert our best efforts to that end.

Library of Congress Cataloging-in-Publication Data
House beautiful entertaining / the editors of House beautiful magazine
    : text by Jane Ellis.
       p. cm.
    Includes index.
    ISBN 0-688-15097-7
    1. Cookery.   2. Entertaining.   I. Ellis, Jane.   II. House beautiful.
TX714.H6813   1997
641.5--dc21   97-21770
                                           CIP

Printed in Great Britain
First Edition
1 2 3 4 5 6 7 8 9 10

EDITED BY DERI REED   DESIGNED BY YOLANDA MONTEZA

PRODUCED BY SMALLWOOD & STEWART, INC., NEW YORK

Table of Contents

1

FIRST IMPRESSIONS

Hors d'Oeuvres   2
Appetizers   18

2

AT TABLE

Soups   34
Salads   46

3

THE MAIN COURSE

Pasta   66
Seafood   80
Poultry   88
Meat   100
Side Dishes   112

SWEET ENDINGS

Desserts   134

PHOTOGRAPHY CREDITS   173

RECIPE INDEX   174

Foreword

What better compliment than to invite someone to dinner? I know there is no gift my wife Jane and I enjoy as much as an invitation to share a meal. It means someone wants to spend some time with us. It is an opportunity to see good friends and a wonderful way to meet new ones. Then there is the sensual pleasure of the food itself, cooked and served in ways we had not imagined. Part of the entertainment, of course, is sitting back and enjoying the creativity of our hosts — the way they serve the drinks, how they set the table, arrange the flowers, plan the menu, and prepare the food.

When the entertaining is at our house, we have, over the years, come to a happy division of the chores: I set the table and arrange the flowers; Jane does the cooking. In the country, we share in the fun of shopping for fresh foods and vegetables; in either the city or the country, we share in the clean-up chores.

Setting the table gives me the pleasure I assume an artist takes in painting a new canvas: choosing the objects, thinking about the colors, the light, the mood we hope to create. Jane takes the same pleasure in planning the menu, often using the occasion to try a new dish. The exceptions, of course, are annual holidays, where we have learned both family members and guests have certain expectations, and traditions are the essence of the occasion.

In the main, entertaining is a wonderful opportunity to extend ourselves, whether as guests or hosts: reaching out to new people, trying new things, celebrating life and friendships in new ways. House Beautiful's food and entertaining editor, Jane Ellis, has spent a lifetime entertaining and being entertained — reporting on the best dinner parties and top restaurants over the years. The hundreds of recipes and entertaining ideas you will find in these pages are the harvest of that bountiful experience. We hope they will entertain you, and help you as you entertain.

LOUIS OLIVER GROPP
Editor in Chief

Introduction

To be entertained is one of life's great pleasures, but to entertain others can be more pleasurable still. Giving parties comes easily for some; for others it's cause for trepidation. But today's relaxed and casual entertaining can mean more fun for everyone.

The pleasure starts with mulling over a menu, thinking about dishes that will delight your guests and fit the occasion. There's no reason to be too ambitious with the food. Years ago, some Boston friends invited me and my husband to dinner, knowing we were dining at Julia Child's the following evening. Wondering how they could possibly compete, they simply decided not to, and came up with a wonderfully zany menu — fried chicken, collard greens, and champagne. It was a delight. It had flare and simplicity. Simplicity always works.

Simple food, especially for parties of twelve or more, is hard to beat. For me, it's shepherd's pie, for Bill Blass, it's meatloaf, for Linda Allard, braised lamb shanks. One or two beautifully executed dishes are always better than a hodgepodge of mediocre ones. Lou Gropp's ideal New Year's Eve dinner is angel hair pasta topped with a scoop of caviar. Elegant, and oh, so simple.

Allow time to enjoy more than just the cooking — setting the table and arranging the flowers are fun too. And with the enormous selection of china, glassware, and linens available today, it's easy to design a table for any occasion.

These are wonderful times to entertain, when so many of the old formalities no longer restrict us. Just look through the pages of House Beautiful Entertaining and be inspired.

JANE ELLIS
Food and Entertaining Editor

FIRST IMPRESSIONS

An open door, a bouquet of flowers, a host relaxed and at ease, good food, and convivial company — these are the ingredients of a successful party. The welcome comes naturally — greetings and introductions as guests gather. Then the overture — glass in hand, everyone unwinds and begins to enjoy the company of new and old friends. Now is the time to offer delicious little bites to sate hunger and stimulate the appetite — hors d'oeuvres, those little "finger foods" that are the mainstay of cocktail parties; and appetizers, small dishes that can also serve as a first course.

Hors d'oeuvres, above all, should be manageable. For the health-conscious, vegetable and salad crudités — asparagus spears or endive leaves, say, with a tangy dip — are always welcome. But as caterer Sean Driscoll finds, the sinful ones are always the first to go, like beggars' purses or salmon tartare. But equally tempting are delicate little mouthfuls like James Beard's onion sandwiches (irresistible to decades of party goers) and Charlie Palmer's elegant Parmesan tuiles.

For appetizers, the choices are much wider. They should delight the eye, stimulate the appetite, and set the tone for the rest of the meal — steamed mussels, cheese soufflé, and *brandade de morue* come to mind.

❖ CHARLIE PALMER'S PARMESAN TUILES

MAKES ABOUT 24 TUILES

12 ounces Parmigiano-Reggiano cheese, grated

Charlie Palmer, owner and chef of New York's three-star restaurant Aureole, makes his savory melt-in-the-mouth tuiles with just one ingredient — grated Parmigiano-Reggiano. Surprisingly easy to make, they are elegant enough to accompany a flute of the best Champagne.

Preheat the oven to 350°F. Place a 3-inch ring mold on a large non-stick baking sheet and sprinkle about 2 tablespoons of the cheese into the mold in an even layer. Repeat to make more tuiles. Bake for 9 to 10 minutes, until golden brown. Immediately remove each tuile with a spatula and place it over a rolling pin, so it makes a curved shape. (The tuiles will become crisp as they cool.) Repeat until all the cheese has been used.

❖ CHARLIE PALMER'S HONEY TUILES

MAKES ABOUT EIGHTEEN 2x6-INCH TUILES

¹/₄ cup (¹/₂ stick) unsalted butter, at room temperature

3 tablespoons honey

2 large egg whites

¹/₂ cup all-purpose flour

¹/₂ cup confectioners' sugar

These crisp honey tuiles are made by brushing batter over a stencil on a cookie sheet, then baking briefly. Try different shapes — stars, diamonds, ovals. Serve them as something sweet with drinks or use them to garnish a fruit dessert or ice cream.

Design a tuile stencil of your choice and cut the shape out of a sheet of thin plastic or cardboard.

Preheat the oven to 300°F. In a bowl with an electric mixer and paddle attachment, whip the butter and honey until smooth. With the mixer on low, slowly add the egg whites, flour, and sugar, mixing until incorporated.

Place the stencil on a nonstick baking sheet. With a spatula, spread a thin layer of batter over the stencil. Repeat the process to make more tuiles. Bake the tuiles for 5 minutes, until golden brown. Immediately remove each tuile with a spatula and place it over a rolling pin, so it makes a curved shape. (The tuiles will become crisp as they cool.) Repeat until all the batter has been used.

❖ CROSTINI WITH FOUR TOPPINGS

MAKES ABOUT 4 DOZEN CROSTINI

Crostini:

Extra-virgin olive oil, for brushing

1 long (28-inch) baguette, sliced on the
diagonal into ½-inch slices

*Crostini — thin slices of baguette, brushed with oil and toasted — make
great finger food when topped with savories. These four winners
come from James O'Shea, owner of the West Street Grill, a celebrated
restaurant in Litchfield, Connecticut. Herb-scented white bean
purée is topped with a strip of red pepper; tuna combined with anchovies
and garlic makes a flavorful paste; Stilton, creamed with olive oil
and brandy, makes a great foil for baked wedges of Bartlett pear; shiitake
mushroom caps are flavored with garlic and herbs.*

Preheat the oven to 375°F. Brush a baking sheet very lightly with
olive oil. Brush both sides of the bread slices with olive oil and place
on the baking sheet in one layer. Bake, turning once, for 10 minutes,
until lightly toasted.

❖ WHITE BEAN PURÉE

MAKES 12 CROSTINI

5 tablespoons extra-virgin olive oil

2 garlic cloves, finely chopped

1 tablespoon finely chopped fresh
flat-leaf parsley

1 teaspoon finely chopped fresh sage
(or ½ teaspoon dried)

1 teaspoon finely chopped fresh thyme
(or ½ teaspoon dried)

1½ cups cooked white beans

Kosher salt and freshly ground black pepper,
to taste

1 teaspoon chili oil

12 Crostini (recipe above)

12 roasted red pepper strips, for garnish

Warm 2 tablespoons of the olive oil in a small skillet over medium
heat. Add the garlic, parsley, sage, and thyme and heat for 3 minutes. Stir in the beans and season with salt and pepper. Cover and
cook for 8 to 10 minutes, until hot. Transfer to a food processor,
add the remaining 3 tablespoons olive oil and the chili oil, and
process until the mixture is smooth; if it seems is too thick, add a
little water. Spread the bean purée on the crostini, garnish each with
a red pepper strip, and serve.

ANCHOÏADE

MAKES 12 CROSTINI

One 2-ounce jar anchovy fillets packed in
   olive oil, drained

1 ounce tuna packed in oil, drained

2 garlic cloves

2 tablespoons extra-virgin olive oil

¼ teaspoon herbes de Provence

1 teaspoon fresh lemon juice, or to taste

1 teaspoon capers, rinsed

12 Crostini (recipe opposite)

In a food processor, combine the anchovies, tuna, garlic, olive oil, and herbes de Provence. Process until the mixture is smooth. Season with the lemon juice. Transfer to a bowl and fold in the capers. Spread a light smear of the anchoïade on the crostini and serve.

STILTON WITH ROASTED PEARS

MAKES 12 CROSTINI

2 firm but ripe Bartlett pears, peeled, halved
   and cored

1 lemon, halved

Melted butter, for brushing

8 ounces Stilton cheese or other blue cheese

2 tablespoons olive oil

2 tablespoons brandy

Freshly ground black pepper, to taste

12 Crostini (recipe opposite)

Preheat the broiler. Lightly butter a baking sheet. Cut each pear half into 3 wedges. Cut each wedge lengthwise into ⅛-inch slices, leaving the stem end intact. Fan the pears on the baking sheet, squeeze lemon juice over them, and brush lightly with butter. Broil until pale brown, about 6 minutes. Remove and set aside.

In a bowl, beat together the Stilton, olive oil, and brandy until smooth. Season with pepper.

Spread the Stilton paste on the crostini and place on a baking sheet. Broil for 1 to 2 minutes, until the tops begin to bubble. Top each crostini with a roasted pear section and serve.

ROASTED SHIITAKE MUSHROOMS

MAKES 12 CROSTINI

12 medium shiitake mushrooms, stemmed

3 tablespoons extra-virgin olive oil, plus more
   for brushing

4 garlic cloves, thinly sliced

1½ teaspoons finely chopped fresh winter
   savory (or ½ teaspoon dried)

2 fresh rosemary sprigs (or 1 teaspoon dried)

½ teaspoon kosher salt

Freshly ground black pepper, to taste

12 Crostini (recipe opposite)

Preheat the oven to 350°F. In a large bowl, combine the mushrooms, olive oil, garlic, savory, rosemary, salt, and pepper. Toss well, being careful not to break the mushroom caps. Spread the mushrooms on a baking sheet or roasting pan and roast for 15 minutes, until nicely browned. Place 1 mushroom cap on top of each crostini, brush with olive oil, and serve.

THAI-SKEWERED CHICKEN

MAKES ABOUT 4 DOZEN HORS D'OEUVRES

Chicken:

1 cup minced lemon grass

2 tablespoons olive oil

2 tablespoons honey

1 onion, thinly sliced

2 jalapeño chile peppers, seeded and sliced
  (wear rubber gloves when handling
  chile peppers)

2 garlic cloves, minced

8 skinless boneless chicken breast halves

1 red bell pepper, cored, seeded, and julienned

8 scallions, green part only

Sauce:

2 tablespoons olive oil

1 cup minced lemon grass

2 garlic cloves, minced

1 cup hoisin sauce

2 cups coconut milk

1 cup finely chopped toasted unsalted peanuts

This is barbecue with a Thai twist from caterer David Ziff: Chicken breasts marinated in chile peppers, lemon grass, honey, and olive oil are baked in the oven. They are delicious served on bamboo skewers and dipped in a coconut-hoisin sauce and chopped peanuts.

To prepare the chicken, combine the lemon grass, olive oil, honey, onion, jalapeños, and garlic in a large bowl. Add the chicken, turning to coat, cover, and refrigerate for 24 hours.

Preheat the oven to 450°F. Remove a chicken breast from the marinade and with a sharp knife, butterfly it by making a horizontal cut into one of the long sides of the breast, and cutting to within $1/2$ inch of the opposite side, keeping the top and bottom layers even in thickness. Place several strips of red pepper and a scallion at one short end of the chicken breast and roll up. Place seam-side down in a baking dish. Repeat with the remaining chicken breasts, red peppers, and scallions.

Bake the chicken rolls for 5 minutes, until cooked through. Remove from the oven and allow to cool. Slice the chicken rolls crosswise into $1/2$-inch pieces and place each on a bamboo skewer.

To prepare the sauce, heat the olive oil in a skillet over medium heat. Add the lemon grass and garlic and sauté for 1 minute. Remove from the heat, add the hoisin sauce and coconut milk, and stir to combine.

Dip the edge of each chicken piece into the sauce and then into the chopped peanuts and serve.

"A handsome setting enhances not just the meal, but the level of conversation as well, for guests will rise to a beautiful occasion," says crafts and textile designer Jack Lenor Larsen. He proves his point with this table: Against a backdrop of ornamental grasses is a rich mix of Philippine baskets, Japanese lacquer, and stoneware vessels, all in place for an oriental feast.

❖ JAMES BEARD'S ONION SANDWICHES

MAKES 16 SANDWICHES

32 slices very thinly sliced white bread

About ½ cup mayonnaise

1 sweet onion, sliced paper thin with
    a mandoline

Salt and freshly ground black pepper, to taste

½ cup minced fresh parsley

*The late great James Beard was always bored by crudités, but he did
love these delicate onion sandwiches, which he invented in the 1930s when
he was a caterer. Make a lot of them — they disappear fast.*

With a round cookie cutter, cut 1 circle out of each slice of bread.
Spread a thin coat of mayonnaise on 1 side of each circle. Place an
onion slice on half of the circles and sprinkle with salt and pepper.
Top with the remaining circles, mayonnaise-side down. Spread a
thin coat of mayonnaise on the edge of each sandwich and roll the
edges in the parsley.

Arrange the sandwiches on a serving platter, cover with a damp
kitchen towel, and refrigerate until ready to serve.

*James Beard was not a lover of vegetable crudités,
but he did approve of this spirited way with tomatoes. Fill a bowl with cherry tomatoes and let guests
dip them first in vodka, then in salt.*

❖ SALMON TARTARE ON SIX-GRAIN BREAD

MAKES 30 HORS D'OEUVRES

1 pound skinless salmon fillets, cut into
     ¹/₄-inch dice

1 heaping tablespoon minced fresh dill, plus
     whole sprigs for garnish

35 juniper berries, finely minced

2 large shallots, finely diced

3 tablespoons fresh lime juice

2 tablespoons light olive oil

Salt and freshly ground black pepper, to taste

1 loaf six-grain bread, crusts removed and cut
     into thirty 1¹/₄-inch-square slices.

Caterers Serena Bass and Stephen Kennard have a way with elegant hors d'oeuvres that are fast and simple to assemble. In this quick canapé, juniper berries and dill are sharp, pungent foils to the richness of salmon tartare.

In a bowl, combine the salmon, minced dill, and juniper berries and refrigerate for at least 1 hour or overnight.

One hour before serving, add the shallots, lime juice, and olive oil to the salmon and mix well. Season with salt and pepper and refrigerate.

To serve, spoon the salmon mixture onto the slices of bread and garnish with dill sprigs.

Clockwise from top: Sea Scallop Ceviche in Radicchio; Root Vegetable Pancakes (page 12); Beet and Apple on Endive; Salmon Tartare on Six-Grain Bread; melon wrapped in prosciutto

❖ SEA SCALLOP CEVICHE IN RADICCHIO

MAKES 30 HORS D'OEUVRES

1 pound very fresh sea scallops

1 cup fresh lime juice (from 8 to 10 limes)

2 medium tomatoes, peeled, seeded, and cut
    into 1/2-inch dice

1 jalapeño chile pepper, seeded and finely
    chopped (wear rubber gloves when
    handling chile peppers)

1 ripe avocado, pitted, peeled, and chopped

1/2 red bell pepper, seeded and chopped

1/4 cup extra-virgin olive oil

3 tablespoons snipped fresh chives

2 tablespoons chopped fresh cilantro

3 radicchio heads, leaves separated, rinsed, and
    dried (about 30 leaves)

*Use only the freshest sea scallops from a source you trust. If you
are not sure they are absolutely fresh, cook them in boiling water until
translucent and halve the marinating time.*

Slice each scallop horizontally into 2 or 3 discs, place in a ceramic or glass bowl with the lime juice, and toss. Cover and refrigerate for at least 5 to 6 hours, or overnight.

About 30 minutes before serving, add the tomatoes, jalapeño, avocado, and red bell pepper to the scallops. Chill well.

Just before serving, add the olive oil, chives, and cilantro to the scallops and stir well. Place the radicchio leaves on a large serving platter and, with a slotted spoon, place 1 tablespoon of the ceviche in each leaf. Serve immediately.

❖ BEET AND APPLE ON ENDIVE

MAKES ABOUT 30 HORS D'OEUVRES

3 Belgian endive heads, leaves separated

1/4 pound beets, washed, stems removed, and
    root ends trimmed

1 Granny Smith apple, peeled, cored, finely
    diced, and tossed with juice of 1 lemon

1 envelope unflavored gelatin

1/4 cup cold water

1/4 cup mayonnaise

Salt and freshly ground black pepper, to taste

*Endive leaves are both hors d'oeuvre and utensil in small bites — like
a spoon, their wide ends hold a sweet, earthy melange of diced fresh beets
and apple. Soaking the endive leaves in cold water will crisp them up.*

Soak the endive leaves in a bowl of cold water for 10 minutes and drain. Cover and refrigerate until needed.

In a saucepan, combine the beets with cold salted water to cover. Bring to a boil and cook, covered, for about 30 minutes, until tender. Drain and let cool slightly. Slip the skins off and dice the beets finely. Combine the beets and apple in a bowl and toss. Set aside.

In a small saucepan, sprinkle the gelatin over the water. Allow the mixture to sit for 5 minutes, until the gelatin is softened. Place the saucepan over low heat and cook, stirring, for about 2 minutes, until the gelatin is melted. Remove from the heat and cool slightly.

In a small bowl, whisk 1 tablespoon of the gelatin mixture into the mayonnaise (reserve the remaining gelatin for another use or discard). Add the mayonnaise to the apple and beets, stir to combine, and season with salt and pepper. Spoon tablespoons of the mixture onto the wide ends of the endive leaves and serve.

ROOT VEGETABLE PANCAKES WITH GINGER DIPPING SAUCE

MAKES ABOUT 30 HORS D'OEUVRES

Sauce:

¼ cup hoisin sauce

¼ cup fresh orange juice

One 2-inch piece fresh ginger, peeled and finely grated

⅛ teaspoon salt

Pancakes:

2 parsnips, peeled

2 carrots, peeled

1 sweet potato, peeled

2 tablespoons butter

1 small yellow onion, minced

1 large egg

1 heaping tablespoon all-purpose flour

2 heaping teaspoons curry powder

½ teaspoon ground red pepper

½ teaspoon freshly ground black pepper

1 tablespoon vegetable oil, or more if needed

Root vegetable pancakes — a colorful take on old-fashioned potato pancakes — are best served piping hot, straight from the pan. They are so good, though, that you'll have a problem getting them out of the pan fast enough.

To prepare the sauce, in a small bowl, combine the hoisin, orange juice, ginger, and salt. Cover and refrigerate. (The sauce can be stored for up to 1 week in the refrigerator. Bring to room temperature and stir well before using.)

To prepare the pancakes, in a food processor fitted with the fine grating disk, separately shred the parsnips, carrots, and sweet potato. Place the vegetables in separate bowls and set aside.

Melt the butter in a large skillet over medium heat. Sauté the onion for about 5 minutes, until softened. Add the carrots and potato and sauté about 5 minutes, until partially done. Add the parsnips and sauté for 3 more minutes. Remove the pan from the heat and stir in the egg, flour, curry powder, red pepper, and black pepper. (The pancake batter can be prepared ahead and refrigerated overnight. Bring to room temperature before continuing.)

Heat the oil in a large nonstick skillet over medium heat. Working in batches, scoop up the batter in well-rounded tablespoons and place in the skillet. Flatten the mounds with the back of a spatula and cook the pancakes, turning once, about 4 minutes, until crisp and golden brown. Serve hot with the dipping sauce on the side.

PRE-DINNER BITES

At a cocktail party, plan on six or seven hors d'oeuvres for each guest; but when serving them as a little something before dinner, just two or three should do. These need not be elaborate — they could be a simple selection of olives with roasted almonds or peanuts.

At parties given by chef Daniel Boulud's catering company, Feasts & Fêtes, hors d'oeuvres are served on trays covered with herbs, grains, sea salt, dried cherries, or beans. This sets off the food delightfully, and keeps trays tidy and easy to replenish.

❖ BEGGARS' PURSES

MAKES ABOUT 4 DOZEN PURSES

Mayonnaise (have all ingredients at room
   temperature):

1 extra-large egg yolk

Salt and freshly ground white pepper, to taste

1 teaspoon rice vinegar

1 teaspoon dry vermouth

1 teaspoon fresh lemon juice

6 tablespoons extra-virgin olive oil

6 tablespoons peanut oil

Filling:

3/4 pound cooked lobster meat, finely chopped

7 ounces fresh black truffles, finely chopped

1/2 cup mayonnaise (recipe above)

1 tablespoon dry vermouth

1 teaspoon fresh lemon juice

Salt and freshly ground black pepper, to taste

Crêpes:

8 extra-large eggs

2 cups plus 2 tablespoons all-purpose flour

3 cups milk

Pinch salt

1 cup (2 sticks) unsalted butter, clarified and still
   liquid

2 bunches long fresh chives, for garnish

Beggars' Purses are the signature hors d'oeuvres of Wayne Nish, chef and co-owner of New York's March restaurant. The elegant bundles are made from super-thin crêpes, filled with lobster and black truffles, then tied with chives. Pass them around on a tray at cocktail time or serve two or three as a first course.

To prepare the mayonnaise, in a medium bowl with an electric mixer, beat the egg yolk until thick and lemon-colored. Season with salt and white pepper. Add $1/2$ teaspoon each of the vinegar, vermouth, and lemon juice and beat well.

Combine the olive oil and peanut oil in a 2-cup measuring cup and add to the egg mixture while beating with a fork, drop by drop at first, then in a gradually increasing amount as the mixture thickens. Slowly add the remaining $1/2$ teaspoon each vinegar, vermouth, and lemon juice and beat well. Cover and refrigerate. Makes about $1^{1}/_{4}$ cups.

To prepare the filling, combine the lobster meat and truffles in a large bowl. Blend in the mayonnaise, vermouth, and lemon juice. Season with salt and pepper. Cover and refrigerate overnight.

To prepare the crêpes, whisk together the eggs, flour, milk, and salt in a large bowl until thoroughly blended. Blend in $1/4$ cup of the clarified butter and allow the batter to rest for at least 20 minutes.

With a paper towel dipped in the remaining butter, rub the bottom of a 5-inch nonstick crêpe pan and heat over medium heat. Ladle in about 2 tablespoons of batter and swirl to cover the bottom of the pan. The crêpe should be almost transparent. Cook until the edges begin to crisp but not brown, about 30 seconds. Transfer to a plate, cooked-side down. Repeat to make about 4 dozen crêpes, stacking them on the plate. (The crêpes can be prepared to this point, covered with plastic wrap, and kept at room temperature for 3 to 4 hours, or refrigerated overnight.)

To assemble the purses, wrap the chives in a damp paper towel and place in a microwave on high power for 10 to 20 seconds, or until limp. Trim the crêpe edges. Place 1 scant tablespoon of the filling in the center of one crêpe. Gather up the crêpe around filling, pleating it, and tie securely with a chive. Repeat with the remaining crêpes, filling, and chives. Serve immediately.

❖ CÉLERI RÉMOULADE

MAKES 30 TO 40 HORS D'OEUVRES

½ pound celeriac, peeled and julienned

1 tablespoon mayonnaise

1 tablespoon Dijon mustard

1½ teaspoons red wine vinegar

1 tablespoon finely chopped cornichons

1 tablespoon finely minced fresh chives

Salt and freshly ground black pepper, to taste

One 6-ounce bag vegetable chips

⅓ cup walnut pieces

Red peppercorns (optional)

Celery root in a mustardy mayonnaise from Daniel Boulud of New York's Daniel restaurant is set on root vegetable chips, the latest version of the classic potato chip. For dramatic presentation, they are served on a tray of red peppercorns.

Cook the celeriac in a medium saucepan of salted boiling water for 5 to 7 minutes, until tender. Drain, cool under cold running water, and drain again.

Combine the celeriac, mayonnaise, mustard, vinegar, cornichons, and chives in a bowl. Season with salt and pepper. Cover the bowl with plastic wrap and refrigerate until ready to serve.

Place a heaping small spoonful of the céleri rémoulade on each vegetable chip and top with a walnut piece. Line a serving tray with red peppercorns, if using, arrange the chips on top, and serve.

Drinks at Six

CHARLIE PALMER'S PARMESAN TUILES (PAGE 3)

JAMES BEARD'S ONION SANDWICHES (PAGE 9)

THAI-SKEWERED CHICKEN (PAGE 7)

CÉLERI RÉMOULADE

MIXED NUTS

ASSORTED OLIVES

CHAMPAGNE

RED WINE

WHITE WINE

MARTINIS

Cocktails

They are the first thing we offer guests after a warm welcome. They can be a prelude to dinner or a party in themselves. A home bar should have the makings of a "cocktail" to please everyone. These days it may well be wine, a spritzer, or sparkling water. But there are always those game for the more tradtional libations, especially on big occasions. Martinis are indeed making a comback, and there is always a new drink, such as the Caipirinha, Brazil's heady blend of cachaça, lime, sugar, and cracked ice (above right).

"The right drink promotes gaiety and lends an aura of risk," says wine and spirits expert William Grimes, who suggests, when only champagne will do, offering sparkling wine cocktails — just as festive and less expensive. The classic champagne cocktail calls for a sugar cube soaked in Angostura bitters adddded to a glass of sparkling wine — a Californian "champagne" or Alsatian cremant. Garnish with a twist of lemon. An even simpler drink is kir royale — sparkling wine with a splash of crème de cassis.

CALVADOS COCKTAIL

-2 ounces Calvados

-2 ounces fresh orange juice

-Dash of Cointreau

-Twist of orange peel

Pour the Calvados, orange juice, and Cointreau into an ice-filled shaker. Shake, then strain into a cocktail glass. Garnish with the orange peel.

LE PERROQUET

-Generous dash of Campari

-Dash of gin

-2 ounces orange juice

-4 ounces chilled champagne

-Twist of lemon and orange peel

Pour the Campari, gin, and orange juice into a champagne flute. Top with champagne. Garnish with the peel.

HOLIDAY MARTINI

-4 ounces lemon vodka

-Dash of Cointreau

-Twist of tangerine or orange peel

Pour the vodka and Cointreau into an ice-filled shaker and shake. Strain into a martini glass. Garnish with tangerine peel.

Cocktails that give a party pizzazz (from left) champagne cocktail, Le Perroquet, and holiday martini. These were concocted at the Rainbow Room by head bartender Dale DeGroff

---

SETTING UP THE BAR

- Choose an area where circulation is easy and open, in order to avoid a bottleneck.
- Don't stint on glasses. Allow for three per guest for a cocktail party. Simple bistro or restaurant supply glasses are fine for all but the most formal gatherings.
- Provide plenty of counter space or little tables covered with a festive cloth so guests can put down empty glasses.
- As a rule of thumb, if you have more than twelve guests you should have bartending help. If there are more than a hundred and twenty guests you should have drinks passed as well as set up bars.

❖ GRILLED VEGETABLE ANTIPASTO WITH CHÈVRE

SERVES 4

1/2 cup olive oil

1/4 cup balsamic vinegar

5 fresh basil leaves, slivered

2 zucchini, halved lengthwise, and flesh scored with a crosshatch pattern

2 summer squash, halved lengthwise and flesh scored with a crosshatch pattern

2 large red onions, cut into 1-inch-thick slices

4 bunches scallions, root ends trimmed and discarded

2 red bell peppers, halved, cored, and seeded

2 yellow bell peppers, halved, cored, and seeded

Two 6-inch-long mini-baguettes, halved lengthwise

1/4 cup chopped fresh parsley

2 tablespoons freshly ground black pepper

One 8-ounce chèvre (goat cheese) log

1/4 cup sun-dried tomatoes packed in oil

4 thick tomato slices

Balsamic Vinaigrette (recipe follows)

Fresh parsley and basil leaves, for garnish

Foster's Market, a specialty food store in Durham, North Carolina, prepares grilled vegetables with the freshest produce available. If you see something at the market that looks just-picked and irresistible, by all means substitute it for any of the vegetables here. Try firing up the barbecue and grilling the vegetables before your guests arrive — they are delicious at room temperature.

Preheat the grill to high and brush with oil. In a small bowl, mix together the olive oil, vinegar, and basil. Brush the zucchini, squash, red onions, scallions, red and yellow peppers, and baguette halves with the olive oil mixture. Grill the vegetables, turning once, for about 5 minutes; the vegetables should still be crunchy and hold their shape. Grill the baguette halves, cut-side down, for 1 to 2 minutes. Set aside.

Mix together the parsley and black pepper on a plate. Roll the chèvre log in it until completely covered. Cut the log into eight 1-inch slices.

Arrange the grilled vegetables, baguette halves, chèvre slices, sun-dried tomatoes, and tomato slices on 4 dinner plates. Lightly drizzle the balsamic vinaigrette on top of the vegetables and garnish the plates with the parsley and basil leaves. Serve the remaining vinaigrette on the side.

BALSAMIC VINAIGRETTE

MAKES ABOUT 1 1/4 CUPS

1/2 cup balsamic vinegar

2 garlic cloves, minced

1 teaspoon freshly ground black pepper

3/4 cup extra-virgin olive oil

10 fresh basil leaves, slivered

Mix together the vinegar, garlic, and pepper in a small bowl. Whisk in the olive oil in a slow steady stream until the vinaigrette thickens. Stir in the basil.

SLOW-ROASTED TOMATOES

SERVES 8 TO 10

4 pounds ripe tomatoes (about 30 plum
tomatoes or 12 to 16 regular tomatoes)
2 tablespoons extra-virgin olive oil
1 teaspoon sugar
1/2 teaspoon salt
Freshly ground black pepper, to taste

Slow roasting is a wonderful technique for concentrating the flavors of tomatoes. For a special first course, serve these intensely flavored little jewels on slices of toasted baguette with a basil leaf for garnish. You can also mash them with herbs to make a quick sauce for pasta or grilled seafood.

Preheat the oven to 325°F. Cut small tomatoes lengthwise in half; quarter larger tomatoes lengthwise. In a medium bowl, toss the tomatoes with 1 1/2 tablespoons of the olive oil. Arrange the tomatoes, cut-side up, on a large baking sheet. Sprinkle with the sugar, salt, and black pepper.

Roast the tomatoes for 2 1/2 to 3 hours, until they have lost most of their liquid and are beginning to brown. They should look like dried apricots, and hold their shape when moved. Cool to room temperature.

Just before serving, brush with the remaining 1/2 tablespoon of the olive oil.

ASPARAGUS WITH ROSEMARY AÏOLI

SERVES 6

1/4 cup extra-virgin olive oil
3 or 4 garlic cloves, unpeeled
2 or 3 fresh rosemary sprigs
1 tablespoon balsamic vinegar
2 cups homemade or store-bought mayonnaise
Grated zest and juice of 1 lemon
Grated zest and juice of 1/2 an orange
Freshly ground black pepper, to taste
2 pounds thick asparagus, trimmed

This room-temperature asparagus, zipped up with an herbal aïoli, is a nice starter for a spring dinner of Braised Lamb Shanks (page 106). It comes from John Schmitt, of the Boonville Hotel in California's Mendocino County.

In a food processor, combine the olive oil, garlic, rosemary, and vinegar. Process for 30 seconds. Let sit for 5 minutes.

Strain the rosemary oil into a large bowl and press on the solids with a spoon to extract all the liquid. Discard the solids. Add the mayonnaise, orange zest and juice, lemon zest and juice, and black pepper and mix well.

In a large pot of boiling water, cook the asparagus, covered, for 3 minutes. Drain and immediately refresh in cold water; drain again.

Divide the asparagus among 6 plates and spoon about 3 tablespoons rosemary aïoli over each serving. (The remaining aïoli will keep for 1 week refrigerated.)

❖ BAY SCALLOPS SAUCE VIERGE

SERVES 6

Sauce vierge:

¹/₂ cup extra-virgin olive oil

2 tablespoons fresh lemon juice

I small tomato, diced

I small red bell pepper, peeled, seeded, and diced

I small yellow bell pepper, peeled, seeded, and diced

I tablespoon chopped fresh basil

I tablespoon chopped fresh tarragon

I tablespoon chopped fresh chives

I tablespoon chopped fresh parsley

Kosher salt and freshly ground black pepper, to taste

Scallops:

¹/₂ cup white wine

I shallot, chopped

I bay leaf

I fresh thyme sprig

Freshly ground black pepper, to taste

36 bay scallops (about ¹/₃ pound)

6 scallop shells

These delicately flavored poached scallops are a favorite of chef Marc Poidevin. Serve them on fan-shaped scallop shells (available in kitchen supply stores) for a beautiful presentation.

To prepare the sauce, in a small bowl, mix together the olive oil and lemon juice. Add the tomato, red pepper, yellow pepper, basil, tarragon, chives, and parsley; mix thoroughly. Season with salt and black pepper and set aside.

To prepare the scallops, in a medium saucepan, combine the wine, shallot, bay leaf, thyme, and black pepper. Bring to a boil, add the scallops, and cook for 1 minute. With a slotted spoon, remove the scallops from the cooking liquid and place 6 in each scallop shell. Top with the sauce and serve immediately.

LIGHTING

Soft lighting is perhaps the most important element in setting the mood and flattering guests. Always have as much candlelight as possible. It can be as simple as votive candles set in demitasse saucers, wrapped with a leaf, or tied with raffia. Candles can be floated in glass containers in a shallow vase and rimmed with fresh flowers. For a more formal look, silver, brass, copper, or glass candlesticks grouped together can make a dramatic arrangement and enhance the play of light. And of course nothing is more seductive than a wood-burning fire.

❖ CORIANDER-CURED SALMON

SERVES 6

½ cup peppercorns

½ cup coriander seeds

1½ pounds kosher salt

¼ cup chopped fresh chives

1 very fresh 1½-pound skinless salmon fillet,
about 1-inch thick, pinbones removed

¼ cup crème fraîche*, for garnish

2 tablespoons chopped fresh parsley, for garnish

2 tablespoons chopped fresh chervil, for garnish

*Crème fraîche is a thick, cultured cream used as a topping for desserts and in other dishes. It is available in specialty food shops, or you can make your own. Combine 1 cup heavy cream and ¼ cup sour cream in a small bowl. Let sit in a warm place for 12 to 14 hours, or overnight, until thickened. Refrigerate until ready to serve.

Salmon, cured at home in salt, pepper, and coriander, goes best with thin slices of toasted baguette (easier to cut when stale or frozen). In this recipe, Wayne Nish of New York's March restaurant cures the salmon for five to six hours and serves it garnished with parsley, chervil, and crème fraîche.

Grind the peppercorns in a blender on high speed for 30 seconds. Add the coriander seeds and process for 30 seconds more.

In a large bowl, combine the peppercorn and coriander mixture with the salt and chives. Place half the mixture in the bottom of a deep glass dish, add the salmon, and pour the remaining salt mixture on top. Cover with plastic wrap and refrigerate for 5 to 6 hours. Remove the salmon from the salt mixture and wipe clean with a cloth. Wrap the salmon in plastic wrap and allow to rest for 15 to 20 minutes in the refrigerator.

Thinly slice the salmon on the diagonal and arrange on 6 plates. Garnish with the crème fraîche, parsley, and chervil and serve.

❖ MUSSELS IN WHITE WINE

SERVES 4

¼ cup (½ stick) butter

4 shallots, minced

1 cup white wine

2 garlic cloves, minced

1 bouquet garni of 1 bay leaf, 1 fresh parsley sprig, and 1 fresh thyme sprig tied together with kitchen string

¼ teaspoon freshly ground black pepper

2 pounds mussels, scrubbed, and debearded

2 tablespoons chopped fresh parsley, for garnish

This dish — Moules Marinières — is the easiest and most popular mussel recipe in France, according to chef Vincent Lange of the Ritz-Escoffier cooking school in Paris. Be sure to provide bowls at the table for discarded mussel shells and a spoon and crusty bread for sopping up the broth.

Melt the butter in a large saucepan over medium heat. Sauté the shallots for 4 to 5 minutes, until wilted. Add the wine, garlic, bouquet garni, and black pepper. Cover and cook gently for 10 minutes. Raise the heat to high and add the mussels. Cover and cook, shaking the pot or stirring from time to time, until all the mussels have opened, about 15 minutes. Discard any mussels that do not open, and the bouquet garni. To serve, divide the mussels and cooking liquid among 4 bowls and garnish with the parsley.

❖ JIMTOWN SEAFOOD COCKTAIL

SERVES 8

¾ pound bay scallops

1 lemon, quartered

1 bay leaf

4 peppercorns

¼ cup olive oil

¾ pound large shrimp, peeled, deveined, and split lengthwise

2 cups fresh tomato juice

Juice of 2 limes

2 cups yellow and red cherry tomatoes

1 cup fresh corn kernels (from about 2 ears corn)

1 ripe avocado, pitted, peeled, and cut into chunks

1 jalapeño chile pepper, seeded, and finely chopped (wear rubber gloves when handling hot peppers)

2 tablespoons finely chopped fresh cilantro

Salt and freshly ground black pepper, to taste

Lime wedges, for garnish

It's hard to decide whether this alluring mix of scallops, shrimp, tomato juice, and vegetables is a cold soup or an unusual salad. The Jimtown Store, a family restaurant in California's Alexander Valley, calls it a seafood cocktail. Serve it as a refreshing summer appetizer, or make it part of a substantial lunch, along with some hearty bread and a tossed salad.

In a medium saucepan, bring 4 cups of water to a boil. Add the scallops, lemon, bay leaf, and peppercorns. Turn off the heat, cover the pan, and let stand for 1 minute. Remove and discard the lemon, bay leaf, and peppercorns. Drain the scallops (they should be opaque) and set aside.

Heat the olive oil in a large skillet over high heat. Sauté the shrimp for about 2 minutes, until just pink. Remove from the heat.

Combine the scallops, shrimp, tomato juice, lime juice, tomatoes, corn, avocado, jalapeño, cilantro, salt, and pepper in a large bowl. Lightly toss and chill for at least 1 hour. (The consistency will be like a soup). Garnish with lime wedges and serve.

❖ BRANDADE DE MORUE

SERVES 6 TO 8

1¼ pounds skinless salt cod

2 cups heavy cream

3 garlic cloves

1 bay leaf

1 fresh thyme sprig

1½ cups olive oil

1¼ pounds russet potatoes, peeled, and cut
    into chunks

Salt and freshly ground black pepper, to taste

Chopped fresh chives, for garnish

Toasted French bread slices

Brandade de Morue, the Provençal combination of salt cod, mashed potatoes, garlic, and olive oil, can be served with toasted French bread as an appetizer, or in a gratin dish as an entrée. If your budget permits, give it the fine taste of Provence by garnishing with sliced black truffles. The recipe comes from Pesce restaurant in Washington, D.C.

Place the salt cod in a bowl of cold water and soak in the refrigerator for at least 36 hours, changing the water every 12 hours. Drain.

In a large saucepan over low heat, combine the cream, garlic, bay leaf, and thyme and bring to a simmer. Add the cod and cook for 1 hour. Pour off the cream and reserve it. Add the olive oil to the saucepan and cook the cod for another 30 minutes. Drain, reserving the oil, and set the cod aside. Discard the garlic and herbs.

In a saucepan over medium heat, combine the reserved cream and the potatoes. Cook for about 20 minutes, until the potatoes are soft. Drain, reserving the cream. Pass the potatoes through a food mill or ricer and set aside.

Put the cod in a bowl of a standing mixer fitted with the paddle attachment and beat until the fish is thoroughly broken up. (Or mash the salt cod in a large bowl with a potato masher). Add the potatoes, ½ cup of the reserved cream, and ½ cup of the reserved olive oil. Mix on medium-high speed until well blended (or mash by hand). Add more of the reserved cream until the desired consistency is reached; the brandade should resemble stiffly mashed potatoes. Season with salt and black pepper. Garnish with the chives and serve with toasted bread.

❖ SHROPSHIRE BLUE CHEESE SOUFFLÉED PUDDINGS

SERVES 8

½ cup (1 stick) butter

½ cup all-purpose flour

2 cups half-and-half

4 ounces Shropshire blue cheese or other top-
   quality blue cheese, crumbled

¼ cup freshly grated Parmesan cheese, plus
   shavings for garnish

8 large egg yolks at room temperature

Salt and freshly ground black pepper, to taste

10 large egg whites at room temperature

Pinch cream of tartar

½ cup heavy cream

Chopped fresh chives, for garnish

Puffed and quivering, soufflés may dazzle the diner, but they can fill the cook with fear. These light and creamy soufflé puddings, however, are fail-safe and stress-free: Cooking them twice guarantees that they won't fall, and making them ahead and popping them in the oven twenty minutes before serving takes away the worry. They are from Tom Rapp of Etats-Unis in New York.

Preheat the oven to 350°F. Melt the butter in a medium saucepan over low heat. Add the flour, stirring constantly until completely incorporated. Slowly stir in the half-and-half. Cook, stirring with a wire whisk, for about 2 minutes, until thickened and smooth. Add the blue cheese and Parmesan and stir until melted. Remove from the heat and beat in the egg yolks one at a time. Transfer to a large bowl and season with salt and black pepper (the mixture should be slightly overseasoned).

In a medium bowl with an electric mixer, beat the egg whites and cream of tartar to soft peaks. Do not overbeat. Carefully fold the egg whites into the cheese mixture. Divide the mixture among 8 buttered 4x2½-inch ramekins, filling them to about ¼ inch from the top. Carefully place the filled ramekins in a shallow roasting pan. Pour enough hot water into the pan to come ¾ inch up the sides of the ramekins. Bake for 40 to 45 minutes, until the tops are set and brown. Remove from the water bath and allow to cool to room temperature. (At this point the puddings can be kept at room temperature for several hours or covered in plastic wrap and refrigerated for up to 2 days.)

To serve, preheat the oven to 400°F. Run a knife around the edges of the puddings. Gently unmold each one into the palm of your hand and place right-side-up on an ovenproof dish. Drizzle 1 tablespoon cream over the top of each soufflé. Bake for 15 to 20 minutes, or until the cream is slightly brown and bubbly. Garnish with Parmesan shavings and fresh chives and serve.

❖ PARSLEY AND CHIVE CORN CAKES WITH FRESH CORN RELISH

SERVES 8 TO 12

3 cups fresh corn kernels (from about 6 ears corn)

1 cup milk

$2/3$ cup all-purpose flour

$2/3$ cup cornmeal

1 teaspoon baking powder

4 large eggs

4 large egg yolks

$1/2$ cup (1 stick) butter, melted

$1/2$ cup finely chopped fresh chives, plus extra for garnish

$1/2$ cup finely chopped fresh parsley

1 teaspoon salt

1 teaspoon freshly ground white pepper

3 tablespoons vegetable oil, or more if needed

1 cup crème fraîche*

Fresh Corn Relish (recipe follows)

*Crème fraîche is a thick cultured cream used as a topping for desserts and in other dishes. It is available in specialty food shops. Or you can make your own crème fraîche by combining 1 cup heavy cream and $1/4$ cup sour cream in a small bowl. Let sit in a warm place for 12 to 14 hours, or overnight, until thickened. Refrigerate until ready to serve.

These corn cakes, topped with crème fraîche, are a specialty of the West Street Grill. In the summer, James O'Shea dresses them up with a refreshing corn relish.

In a food processor, combine the corn and milk. Process until the mixture is simultaneously chunky and creamy. Pour into a large bowl, add the flour, cornmeal, and baking powder and mix well.

In a small bowl, beat the eggs, egg yolks, and butter until smooth and frothy. Add to the corn mixture and combine thoroughly. Mix in the chives and parsley and season with the salt and pepper.

Heat the oil in a large skillet over medium-high heat. Working in batches, with a $1\frac{1}{2}$-ounce ladle, scoop up the batter and ladle into the hot oil. Fry the corn cakes for about 2 minutes per side, until golden. Garnish with chives, and serve with the crème fraîche and Fresh Corn Relish.

FRESH CORN RELISH

MAKES ABOUT 2 CUPS

1 cup fresh corn kernels (from about 2 ears corn)

2 tablespoons finely diced carrot

2 tablespoons finely diced red onion

2 tablespoons finely diced celery

2 tablespoons finely diced red bell pepper

3 tablespoons olive oil

2 tablespoons cider vinegar

$1/4$ cup minced fresh chives

Salt and freshly ground black pepper, to taste

In a large pot of salted boiling water, blanch the corn, carrot, onion, celery, and bell pepper for 1 to 2 minutes. Drain and immediately refresh in cold water. Drain the vegetables and place in a medium bowl. Add the olive oil, vinegar, and chives. Toss well and season with salt and black pepper. Cover and refrigerate for at least 2 hours for the flavors to blend.

When decorator Bunny Williams teams up with close friend John Rosselli to prepare dinner parties at her country house, the division of labor is clear: She sets the scene, he does the cooking.

Williams, an inveterate collector, has only to open the doors of her closets to find the makings of spectacular table settings. Antique crystal, china, and porcelain turn her nineteenth-century pedestal dining table into a stunning tableau whenever friends come over. She loves to use richly colored tapestries or Indian bedspreads instead of fancy tablecloths. She sets the table with a free mix of china from those prodigious cupboards.

Flowers offer more visual excitement. Williams's strategy for arranging them on the table is simple: "Stick to a monochromatic palette. Purples and lavenders, say, look better than a whole spectrum of color." Often she tucks some of her smaller collectibles — nineteenth-century porcelain fruits are particular favorites — around the place settings.

And the food? Rosselli's idea of a country dinner is "a simple meal and a good dessert." He is partial to Southern cuisine, and his Roasted Chicken (page 90) and Grits Soufflé (page 115) are favorites among their friends. He never spends more than two hours in preparation, and virtually everything is cooked ahead of time in dishes that can go straight to the table. By the time guests arrive, the table sparkles, the kitchen is immaculate, and the two friends are ready to relax and join their guests in a cocktail.

AT TABLE

*S*oups and salads are just about perfect starters. They can be made ahead of time and warmed up or dressed at the last minute. For a sit-down meal, a cold first course like chilled soup, a composed salad, smoked salmon, or shrimp can already be on the table. A hot soup or hot first course should be served after guests are seated.

Rich, hearty offerings like lentil soup and smoked haddock chowder are wonderfully warming on cold evenings. A light consommé — butternut, perhaps — is an excellent prelude to an elaborate entrée. And in summer there is nothing more delightful or colorful than starting a meal with a delicate cup of cool gazpacho.

Like soups, salads — especially those that include shellfish or smoked fish — can start off a meal, or they can be the main course at lunch or an informal dinner. A green salad can also be served at the end of the meal as a palate cleanser or together with cheese — organic greens or arugula with a light toss of vinaigrette is always good. Staples of summer entertaining, salads — everything from Tuscan bread salad to couscous salad to grilled bean salad — are an essential part of buffets, picnics, barbecues, and casual get-togethers.

JONAH CRAB SOUP WITH WINTER VEGETABLES

SERVES 6

Soup:

3 Jonah or rock crabs (have the fishmonger kill the crabs and discard the gills and intestines)

2 tablespoons butter, preferably clarified

1 tablespoon vegetable oil

1/2 onion, diced

1/2 celery stalk, diced

1/2 carrot, diced

1/4 cup chopped fresh parsley

2 garlic cloves, crushed

2 bay leaves

1 teaspoon peppercorns

2 tablespoons tomato paste

8 cups heavy cream

Ground red pepper, to taste

Salt and freshly ground black pepper, to taste

Garnish:

2 parsnips, peeled and julienned

2 carrots, julienned

1 cup chopped broccoli rabe

At the Mayflower Inn in Connecticut, this hearty soup is served as a prelude to a Thanksgiving feast. Embellished with winter vegetables, it's a warming starter for any special cold-weather dinner.

To prepare the soup, chop the crabs into small pieces. Heat the butter and oil in a large heavy pot over high heat. Sauté the crabs for 10 minutes. Add the onion, celery, carrot, parsley, and garlic and sauté for about 5 minutes, until the onions are translucent and all the vegetables are tender. Add the bay leaves, peppercorns, tomato paste, and cream. Bring to a boil and immediately reduce the heat to low. Simmer for 1 hour, occasionally skimming the surface with a large spoon to remove any foam.

Strain the soup, discarding the solids. Season with red pepper, salt, and black pepper. (The soup can be prepared to this point and refrigerated overnight. Gently reheat before serving.)

To prepare the garnish, in a saucepan of salted boiling water, blanch the parsnips and carrots for 2 minutes. Remove with a slotted spoon, refresh in cold water, and drain. Blanch the broccoli rabe, drain, refresh, and drain again.

Add the parsnips, carrots, and broccoli rabe to the soup and serve immediately.

❖ SMOKED HADDOCK CHOWDER

SERVES 8

¹/₄ cup unsalted butter

1 large onion, thinly sliced

1 pound smoked haddock

2 cups milk

2 cups fish broth, preferably homemade

3 pounds potatoes, peeled and diced

2 cups heavy cream

Juice of ¹/₂ lemon

Freshly ground black pepper, to taste

¹/₄ cup barley

1 cup water

8 thin slices smoked salmon, cut into
  ¹/₄-inch strips

2 tablespoons chopped fresh chives

This chowder comes from the Countess Sheila de Rochambeau, who offers seminars on the art of entertaining at her home in Ballachrochan, in the Scottish Highlands. With prodigious amounts of potatoes, smoked haddock, and smoked salmon, it could be a meal in itself.

Melt the butter in a large heavy pot over low heat. Add the onion, cover and cook, stirring occasionally, for 20 minutes, without browning. Cut three quarters of the haddock into small pieces and add to the pot. Add the milk and broth, raise the heat to medium, and simmer gently for 5 minutes. With a slotted spoon, transfer the haddock to a bowl and set aside.

Add the potatoes to the pot and simmer for about 10 minutes, until tender. Return the cooked fish to the pot and add the cream, lemon juice, and pepper. Transfer to a food processor and process until smooth. Return the mixture to the pot and set aside.

Meanwhile, combine the barley with the water in a small saucepan, bring to a simmer, and cook until tender but not mushy, 30 to 45 minutes.

Bring the fish mixture to a simmer over low heat, and add the cooked barley. Cut the remaining haddock into strips and add to the chowder. Simmer for 5 minutes. Add the smoked salmon and cook for 2 minutes more. Transfer the chowder to a tureen, garnish with the chives, and serve.

THE RIGHT PLACE

Place cards — handwritten by children, or painted on leaves, little fans, seashells, or luggage tags — speed seating, especially when there are more than eight guests. They also enable the host to create a sociable mix.

"To make guests happy, you have to provoke conversation," says John Loring, who seats guests between someone they know and someone they don't, but with whom there will be a subject in common.

❖ LEEK AND FENNEL SOUP

SERVES 6

3 tablespoons olive oil

2 leeks, sliced and well washed

1 fennel bulb, sliced

1 large garlic clove, minced

6 cups water

2 bay leaves, preferably fresh

Salt and freshly ground black pepper, to taste

1/2 cup finely diced zucchini, yellow squash, carrot, and/or red bell pepper, for garnish

3 tablespoons chopped fresh chervil, for garnish

3 tablespoons chopped fresh lemon balm, for garnish (optional)

The sweet essence of two herbs — chervil, with its delicate anise-like tang, and lemon balm, with its hint of mint — enhances the flavors of this soup from the West Street Grill. The herbs are added at the last minute: The heat of the soup extracts their delicate flavors in the time it takes to bring the soup to the table.

Heat the olive oil in a large heavy saucepan over low heat. Stir in the leeks, fennel, and garlic. Cover, and cook, stirring often, for 15 to 20 minutes, until tender.

Raise the heat to medium, add the water and bay leaves, and season with salt and pepper. Bring to a simmer, reduce the heat to low, and simmer for 25 minutes. Discard the bay leaves and transfer the soup to a food processor. Process until puréed. The soup should be light and creamy in texture.

Pour the soup into soup bowls, garnish with the diced vegetables, chervil, and lemon balm, if using, and serve.

❖ MUSHROOM-BARLEY SOUP

SERVES 4

1/2 cup pearl barley

4 cups strong beef broth

6 tablespoons butter

1/2 pound white mushrooms, sliced

1/2 cup minced onions

1/4 cup chopped fresh flat-leaf parsley

Mushroom-barley soup is a wonderful cold-weather comforter — simple and delicious with the essential uncluttered flavors of mushrooms and barley. It comes from food writer Cecille Lamalle.

Bring 4 cups of water to a boil in a medium saucepan. Add the barley, return to a boil, and reduce the heat to low. Simmer for 30 minutes, or until the barley is just barely tender. Drain and set aside.

Bring the broth to a simmer in a large saucepan. In a large skillet over low heat, melt 4 tablespoons of the butter. Sauté the mushrooms and onions, stirring occasionally, for 10 to 15 minutes, until the mushrooms have released their juices. Add the mushrooms and onions to the broth, stir in the barley, and simmer for 30 to 45 minutes, until the barley is tender.

Just before serving, stir in the remaining 2 tablespoons butter and the parsley. Ladle into soup bowls and serve.

Dressing the Table

A beautifully dressed table, whether simple or lavish, gives pleasure all through a party. Flowers, fruits, plants, herbs, and decorative serving pieces can all bring a table to life.

In a riot of color or in a subtle palette of pastels, flowers never fail to delight, from a single unassuming daisy at each place setting to a voluptuous centerpiece of pink peonies in June. A formal dinner might call for orchids and roses; for an informal gathering indoors or out, enamel pitchers filled with sunflowers, earthenware bowls brimming with wildflowers, or a clutch of potted herbs do the trick.

Topiaries and soaring arrangements of flowers add drama and scale to oversize rooms. Tiny pots of pansies scattered over the table can fill a large expanse of wood. A cluster of potted herbs gives a splash of

silvery green and a lovely fragrance to an informal supper. Silver baby cups, tiny cream jugs, and wine decanters can be filled with little nosegays. Seashells and shallow bowls can float a single perfect bloom.

A world of imaginative centerpieces lies beyond flowers. Cachepots and epergnes, cake stands and tureens filled with fruits and vegetables can become memorable table decorations. A mound of tight green artichokes, vel-vety mushrooms, pink-tinged turnips, or polished apples make lovely centerpieces one night, dinner the next. Little boxes of raspberries or red currants straight from the farmstand lend a casual, unexpected dash of color.

And for the winter holidays, a lavishly iced gingerbread house, dwarf firs, rosemary topiaries, clove-studded oranges, bowls of silver and gold balls, all are guaranteed to make table magic.

❖ ESCAROLE AND WHITE BEAN SOUP

SERVES 4 TO 6

1 cup dried cannellini or other white beans, rinsed and picked over

4 cups chicken broth, preferably homemade

1/2 escarole head (or 1/2 pound spinach), tough stalks discarded, washed, and coarsely chopped

8 garlic cloves, chopped

Salt and freshly ground black pepper, to taste

1/4 cup butter or olive oil, or to taste

A southern Italian staple for generations, escarole and white bean soup provides an interesting contrast of flavor and color: creamy, mellow white beans versus the slightly bitter green of escarole. Baby lima, Great Northern, or navy beans can all be used. If escarole is hard to find, try spinach; just don't cook it as long.

Place the beans in a large pot with cold water to cover. Bring to a boil and boil for 1 minute. Cover, remove from the heat, and let stand for at least 1 hour. Drain.

Cover the beans with 3 inches of water and bring to a boil. Reduce the heat to low, cover, and simmer for 1 to 1 1/2 hours, until tender but not soft. Drain.

Combine the broth, escarole, and garlic in a large heavy pot over medium-high heat. Bring to a boil, reduce the heat to low, and simmer for 1 hour (30 minutes if using spinach). Stir in the beans, season with salt and pepper, and bring just to a simmer. Stir in the butter and serve.

❖ GAZPACHO

SERVES 8 TO 10

3 pounds ripe tomatoes, seeded and coarsely chopped

6 red bell peppers, cored, seeded, and coarsely chopped

1 cucumber, peeled and coarsely chopped, plus 1/2 cucumber, diced, for garnish

1/2 onion, coarsely chopped

2 garlic cloves, smashed

2 to 3 tablespoons red wine vinegar

Pinch sugar

Ground red pepper, to taste

Salt and freshly ground black pepper, to taste

Sour cream, for garnish

Chopped fresh chives, for garnish

Seventy varieties of vegetables grow in Raymond Blanc's garden at the Manoir Aux Quat' Saisons, near Oxford, England. One of the most celebrated chefs in England (his restaurant has two Michelin stars), Blanc has a way with vegetables and fruits that rates most highly with his guests. His gazpacho, garnished with chopped chives, diced cucumber, and sour cream, is the essence of summer.

In a food processor, combine the tomatoes, bell peppers, chopped cucumber, onion, and garlic. Process until very finely puréed. Strain through a very fine sieve or put through the finest disk of a food mill. Season with the vinegar, sugar, red pepper, salt, and black pepper. Cover and refrigerate for 2 to 3 hours, until ice-cold.

Ladle the gazpacho into individual bowls, garnish with the sour cream, chives, and diced cucumbers, and serve.

❖ BLACK BEAN GAZPACHO

SERVES 8 TO 10

1 pound dried black beans, rinsed and
    picked over

1 pound dried chick peas, rinsed and
    picked over

4 to 5 pounds ripe tomatoes, peeled, seeded,
    and diced (or two 28-ounce cans crushed
    tomatoes)

4 large green and/or red bell peppers, cored,
    seeded, and coarsely chopped

3 large cucumbers, peeled, seeded, and chopped

2 large Vidalia or red onions, quartered

8 garlic cloves

1/2 cup chopped fresh cilantro

1/2 cup chopped fresh parsley

1/2 cup chopped fresh chives

1/2 cup chopped fresh basil

1 tablespoon chopped canned jalapeño chile
    pepper

1/3 cup balsamic vinegar

Juice of 2 lemons or limes

2 tablespoons ground cumin

1 teaspoon salt, or more to taste

Pinch ground red pepper, or more to taste

At the farmers' market on Block Island, Leslie Hartnett's black bean gazpacho is the first thing on her decorative stand to be snapped up by cottagers (summer people), islanders (year-rounders), and vacationers. A heady mix of black beans and chick peas, it has summery accents of tomatoes, bell peppers, and cucumbers.

Place the beans and chick peas in 2 separate pots with cold water to cover. Bring to a boil and boil for 1 minute. Cover, remove from the heat, and let stand for at least 1 hour. Drain.

Cover the beans and chick peas with at least 3 inches of water and bring to a boil. Reduce the heat to low, cover, and simmer for 1 to 1¹/₂ hours, or until tender but not soft.

Drain the beans and chick peas in a colander, rinse under cold water, and place in a large bowl. Add the tomatoes and set aside.

In a food processor, combine the bell peppers, cucumbers, onions, and garlic. Process until minced. Add to the bean-tomato mixture. Add the cilantro, parsley, chives, basil, jalapeño, vinegar, lemon juice, cumin, salt, and ground red pepper and mix very well. Refrigerate for 2 to 3 hours, until chilled, or overnight. Mix well, taste to correct the seasoning, and serve.

❖ ROASTED RED PEPPER SOUP

SERVES 4 TO 6

12 red bell peppers

1/4 cup olive oil

6 or 7 large onions, cut into 1/4-inch slices

3 or 4 garlic cloves, minced

4 cups chicken broth, preferably homemade

1 small dried chile pepper

Salt, to taste

Garlic Crostini (recipe follows)

Freshly grated Parmesan cheese, for garnish

This spicy soup can be made with store-bought roasted red peppers or fresh peppers, which can be roasted a day ahead of time. Designer Linda Allard serves the soup in colorful bowls and garnishes them with garlic crostini topped with shreds of Parmesan cheese.

Roast the peppers over a gas or charcoal flame, or under a broiler, turning occasionally, for 15 minutes, until blackened on all sides. Transfer to a plastic bag, seal tightly, and steam for 10 minutes. When cool enough to handle, peel, core, and seed the peppers. Reserve any juices.

Heat the olive oil in a large heavy pot over low heat. Add the onions and garlic and sauté, stirring occasionally, for about 30 minutes, until the onions are golden brown. Add the broth, the bell peppers and any juice, and the chile, raise the heat to medium, and bring to a boil. Reduce the heat to low and simmer for 30 minutes, until the vegetables are very soft.

Remove the chile and transfer the soup to a food processor. Process until puréed. Return the soup to the pot, season with salt, and simmer for 15 minutes. Ladle the soup into individual bowls, garnish with the crostini and Parmesan, and serve.

GARLIC CROSTINI

MAKES ABOUT 2 DOZEN CROSTINI

1 baguette, cut into 1/4-inch slices

1/4 to 1/3 cup olive oil

1 to 2 garlic cloves, halved

Chopped fresh parsley

Preheat the oven to 400°F. Brush the bread slices on both sides with olive oil and place on a large baking sheet. Bake, turning once, for 5 to 10 minutes, until golden. Rub the toasts with the garlic and sprinkle with parsley. Serve hot or at room temperature.

❖ LENTIL SOUP WITH SAGE CRÈME FRAÎCHE

SERVES 6

¼ cup olive oil

1 carrot, finely diced

1 leek, white part only, finely diced and well washed

2 celery stalks, finely diced

2 large shallots, minced

1 small garlic head, cloves separated, peeled, and crushed

¼ cup chopped fresh flat-leaf parsley

1½ cups dried lentils, rinsed and soaked in cold water for 2 to 3 hours

8 cups chicken broth or water, heated to a simmer

Salt and freshly ground black pepper, to taste

¼ cup tarragon vinegar

½ cup crème fraîche* or sour cream

8 to 10 fresh sage leaves (or 1 teaspoon dried)

Chopped fresh chervil, for garnish

*Crème fraîche is a thick, cultured cream used as a topping for desserts and in other dishes. It is available in specialty food shops, or you can make your own. Combine 1 cup heavy cream and ¼ cup sour cream in a small bowl. Let sit in a warm place for 12 to 14 hours, or overnight, until thickened. Refrigerate until ready to serve.

Henry Meer of New York City's Cub Room restaurant believes that there is nothing better on a cold day than a hearty, warming soup. He uses root vegetables and lentils for this soup and garnishes it with crème fraîche and a little chervil.

Heat the olive oil in a Dutch oven or a large heavy pot over medium heat. Add the carrot, leek, celery, shallots, garlic, and parsley and sauté for 5 minutes, until softened.

Drain the lentils and add them to the pot along with the broth. Bring to a boil, reduce the heat to low, cover and simmer, stirring frequently, for about 30 minutes, until the lentils are tender but not mushy. Season with salt and pepper, stir in the vinegar, and remove from the heat.

In a food processor, combine the crème fraîche and sage and process until smooth. Ladle the soup into soup bowls, garnish with the crème fraîche and chervil, and serve.

❖ BUTTERNUT CONSOMMÉ

SERVES 6

6 tablespoons unsalted butter

1 onion, thinly sliced

2 medium butternut squash, halved lengthwise,
   then crosswise, peeled, and seeded

8 cups water

Salt and freshly ground black pepper, to taste

1 leek, white part only, split and well washed

2 large egg whites

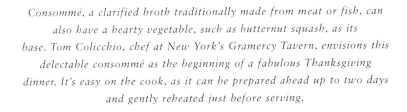

Consommé, a clarified broth traditionally made from meat or fish, can also have a hearty vegetable, such as butternut squash, as its base. Tom Colicchio, chef at New York's Gramercy Tavern, envisions this delectable consommé as the beginning of a fabulous Thanksgiving dinner. It's easy on the cook, as it can be prepared ahead up to two days and gently reheated just before serving.

Melt 2 tablespoons of the butter in a large skillet over low heat. Sauté the onion for 4 to 5 minutes, until translucent. Remove from the heat and set aside.

Set aside the squash bottoms and cut the stem ends into 1-inch cubes. Melt the remaining 4 tablespoons butter in a large pot over medium heat. Sauté the squash cubes, turning occasionally, for 10 to 15 minutes, until lightly browned. Add the onion and water and bring to a gentle simmer. Reduce the heat to low, skim the foam from the top, and simmer for 1¹/₂ hours. Strain and let cool. Season with salt and pepper.

In a food processor, process the leek and 2 of the remaining squash bottoms until finely chopped. Add the egg whites and pulse to blend. Whisk the mixture into the cool stock. Bring the broth to a gentle simmer over low heat, whisking occasionally. Once the egg-white mixture comes to the surface, stop whisking. Simmer for 30 minutes.

Gently remove the egg white mixture with a slotted spoon or spatula. Strain the consommé through double layer of cheesecloth or a piece of muslin set in a strainer. (The consommé may be prepared to this point, cooled, covered, and refrigerated for up to 3 days. When reheating, warm it slowly, being careful not to boil vigorously.)

Meanwhile, cut the remaining squash bottoms into small cubes. In a large pot of salted boiling water, cook the squash 8 to 10 minutes, until softened. Drain. Ladle the consommé into 6 soup bowls, garnish with the squash cubes, and serve.

❖ PASSION FRUIT SOUP

SERVES 6

Garnish:

4 fresh sage leaves

1 large egg white, lightly beaten

1 teaspoon sugar

Soup:

1 cup water

1 cup frozen passion fruit purée

1 cup sugar

2 oranges, peeled and sectioned

2 very ripe passion fruits, halved and pulp
    scooped out

1 mango, peeled, pitted, and scooped into balls

1/2 cup passion fruit sorbet

Intensely perfumed with an aroma like jasmine, gardenias, honey, and lemon, passion fruit appears in this refreshing dessert soup in three forms: sorbet, purée, and fresh. It's a delightful palate-cleanser after a hot and spicy entrée. The recipe comes from Patrice Caillot, pastry chef at Osteria Del Circo in Manhattan.

To prepare the garnish, brush the sage leaves with the egg white and sprinkle lightly with the sugar. Place the leaves on a piece of parchment paper and let dry overnight.

To prepare the soup, in a medium saucepan over medium-high heat, combine the water, passion fruit purée, and sugar and bring to a boil. Remove the pan from the heat and allow to cool. Transfer to a medium bowl, cover with plastic wrap, and refrigerate until chilled.

Divide the orange sections, passion fruit pulp, and mango balls among four chilled shallow soup bowls. Ladle the chilled soup into the bowls and place a small spoonful of sorbet in the middle of each. Garnish with the crystallized sage leaves and serve.

Salads

❖ AVOCADO, PINK GRAPEFRUIT, AND ORANGE SALAD WITH LEMON-PEPPER DRESSING

SERVES 8

Juice of 1 lemon

2 tablespoons fresh pink grapefruit juice

½ cup olive oil

Salt and freshly ground black pepper, to taste

1 avocado, pitted, peeled, and thinly sliced
    lengthwise

2 oranges, peeled, pith removed, and thinly
    sliced crosswise

2 pink grapefruit, peeled, pith removed,
    quartered lengthwise, and thinly sliced
    crosswise

½ cup thinly sliced celery hearts including
    leaves (optional)

¼ cup seasonal berries

Joe Famularo serves this salad for friends at his Key West home. The dressing can be prepared ahead, but don't combine it with the citrus until just before serving.

To prepare the dressing, in a small bowl, combine the lemon and grapefruit juices. Slowly whisk in the olive oil. Season with salt and a liberal amount of pepper. (The dressing can be prepared to this point and refrigerated overnight. Bring the dressing to room temperature before continuing.)

Arrange the avocado in a shallow bowl. Spoon 2 tablespoons of the dressing over the avocado slices, turning them gently to coat. Cover tightly and refrigerate until ready to serve.

To serve, arrange the orange slices in a circle the center of a large platter, overlapping them slightly. Arrange the grapefruit slices around the oranges, overlapping them. Place the avocado slices on top of the orange slices and scatter the celery and berries over them. Spoon the remaining dressing over the salad and serve.

❖ GREEK VILLAGE SALAD

SERVES 4 TO 6

3 small cucumbers, cut into ½-inch slices

3 tomatoes, quartered

1 small red onion, thinly sliced

½ teaspoon salt

¼ teaspoon freshly ground black pepper

¼ cup extra-virgin olive oil

1 tablespoon red wine vinegar

1 tablespoon fresh lemon juice

2 garlic cloves, minced

1 teaspoon dried oregano

4 ounces feta cheese, crumbled (about ½ cup)

½ cup Kalamata olives, pitted

Chef Barbara Fenner serves this salad at the Outermost Inn on Martha's Vineyard. It's an exceptionally delicious way to use tomatoes and cucumbers from the vegetable garden.

In a large salad bowl, combine the cucumbers, tomatoes, and onions. Season with salt and pepper.

In a small bowl, whisk together the olive oil, vinegar, lemon juice, garlic, and oregano. Stir in the feta cheese and olives. Pour the dressing over the vegetables and toss well. Cover and refrigerate for at least 1 hour before serving.

❖ SUMMER SALAD

SERVES 4 TO 6

¹/₂ cup extra-virgin olive oil

¹/₄ cup balsamic vinegar

2 teaspoons anchovy paste

2 garlic cloves, minced

2 teaspoons chopped fresh basil

6 cups summer lettuces, washed, dried, and torn

2 cups yellow pear and red cherry
    tomatoes, halved

*Barbara Smith loves to entertain at her waterfront home in
Sag Harbor, New York. The vinaigrette for this yellow pear and red
cherry tomato salad is enlivened with anchovy paste. Try a
combination of watercress, endive, and mesclun — just about anything
that is fresh, tender, and crisp will do.*

In a large salad bowl, whisk together the olive oil, vinegar, anchovy paste, garlic, and basil. Add the greens and tomatoes, toss gently, and serve.

❖ ORGANIC HERB SALAD WITH BALSAMIC VINAIGRETTE

SERVES 6

1¹/₂ cups extra-virgin olive oil

¹/₄ cup balsamic vinegar

1 small shallot, minced

1 small garlic clove, minced

6 to 8 cups mixed organic baby lettuces and
    herbs, such as butter lettuce, lollo rossa, red
    oak leaf, mizuna, red mustard, garlic chive
    blossoms, dill tops, and sweet cecily leaves
    and seeds

Sea salt and freshly ground black pepper, to taste

Rosemary flowers, meadow sage flowers or
    fresh cilantro flowers, for garnish (optional)

*The enormous variety of organic greens available these days
make the most sensational salads, like this one from the West Street Grill.
Use whichever baby greens you find at your local market.
Let the dressing stand at room temperature for two to four hours for a
more robust vinaigrette.*

In a small bowl, whisk together the olive oil, vinegar, shallot, and garlic. Cover and let stand at room temperature for 2 to 4 hours to heighten the flavors.

    Combine the baby lettuces and herbs in a large chilled glass bowl and toss gently. Quickly whisk the vinaigrette, pour over the salad, and toss. Season with salt and pepper, garnish with the flowers, if using, and serve immediately.

❖ TUSCAN BREAD SALAD

SERVES 6 TO 8

1 pound crusty Tuscan bread (preferably ½ pound white and ½ pound whole wheat), several days old, cut into large chunks

6 cups cold water

½ cup red wine vinegar

1 red onion, cut into ½-inch pieces

8 scallions, white part only, cut into ½-inch pieces

3 very large ripe tomatoes, halved, seeded, and cut into 2-inch pieces

8 anchovy fillets packed in oil, drained and cut into small pieces

15 large fresh basil leaves, torn into thirds, plus 15 whole leaves for garnish

Salt and freshly ground black pepper, to taste

¾ cup olive oil

3 large eggs, hard-boiled and quartered (optional)

Giuliano Bugialli's cooking school in Florence has been a mecca for cooks for over twenty years. Panzanella — Tuscan bread salad — is offered to students during class to keep their energy and spirits up. It's a wonderful way to use stale crusty bread and excess summer tomatoes. Anchovy fillets add additional zip.

Place the bread in a large bowl, add the water and vinegar, and soak for 30 minutes. In a small bowl, soak the onion and scallions in cold water to cover for 30 minutes.

Place the tomatoes and anchovies in a large ceramic or glass serving bowl. Squeeze the liquid out of the bread and put on top of the tomatoes; do not mix. Drain the onion and scallions and put on top of the bread. Sprinkle the torn basil over the top. Cover the bowl with plastic wrap and refrigerate for at least 30 minutes.

Season the salad with salt and pepper, drizzle with the olive oil, and toss well. Garnish with the whole basil leaves. Arrange the hard-boiled eggs on top of the salad, if using, and serve.

❖ HARICOTS VERTS AND WATER CHESTNUT SALAD

SERVES 4

1 pound haricots verts (or tender young green beans)

⅓ cup sesame oil or extra-virgin olive oil

3 tablespoons white wine vinegar or fresh lemon juice

1 tablespoon dry sherry

1 tablespoon honey

1 to 2 teaspoons soy sauce, or to taste

2 teaspoons finely chopped fresh ginger

Salt and freshly ground black pepper, to taste

¼ teaspoon ground red pepper (optional)

12 fresh water chestnuts, peeled and thinly sliced

1 tablespoon finely chopped fresh mint or cilantro, for garnish

Thinly sliced water chestnuts add a nice crunch to this green bean salad dressed with an Asian-inspired vinaigrette. If you can't find haricots verts, tender young string beans can be substituted. This recipe comes from Emalee Chapman.

Bring 4 cups of water to a boil in a large skillet over high heat. Add the beans and cook for 5 to 6 minutes, until tender but still slightly crunchy. Drain and spread on a platter to cool slightly.

In a small bowl, whisk together the oil, vinegar, sherry, honey, and soy sauce. Whisk in the ginger. Season with salt and pepper and red pepper, if desired.

In a large salad bowl, toss the beans with the water chestnuts. Quickly whisk the dressing, pour over the beans and water chestnuts, and toss. Garnish with the mint and serve.

❖ SALAD OF ENDIVE, ORANGE, AND BEETS WITH BEET VINAIGRETTE

SERVES 4

Vinaigrette:

1 medium beet, cooked, peeled, and quartered

1 teaspoon mustard

1/4 cup extra-virgin olive oil

Salt and freshly ground black pepper, to taste

Salad:

2 large beets, cooked, halved, and sliced into
    half-moons

2 oranges, peeled, seeded, and separated into
    sections

4 small Belgian endive heads, halved lengthwise
    and thinly sliced

Fresh parsley and chervil leaves, for garnish

Gérard Vié created this salad for the spa menu at Les Trois Marches in the Trianon Palace at Versailles, France. Large beets take almost an hour to cook in boiling water, small beets about half an hour. They can also be roasted in a 375°F oven for one hour.

To prepare the vinaigrette, place the beet in a food processor and process to a coarse purée. Strain through a fine strainer, pressing with a spoon to extract the juice. Reserve 2 tablespoons of the juice and discard the solids.

In a small bowl, whisk together the beet juice and the mustard. Slowly whisk in the olive oil and season with salt and pepper.

To prepare the salad, arrange the beet slices and orange sections on salad plates. Mound the endive in the center and drizzle a generous amount of beet vinaigrette around the edge of each plate. Garnish with parsley and chervil leaves and serve.

❖ TOMATO, RED ONION, AND MINT SALAD

SERVES 4

Mint oil:

1 bunch fresh mint, stems removed

1/4 cup extra-virgin olive oil

Vinaigrette:

2 tablespoons sherry vinegar

1 tablespoon lemon juice

1 shallot, minced

1 garlic clove, minced

1/4 cup extra-virgin olive oil

Salt and freshly ground black pepper, to taste

3 ripe beefsteak tomatoes or 6 ripe plum
    tomatoes, thinly sliced

1 red onion, thinly sliced

1/4 cup pine nuts, toasted

12 fresh mint leaves, finely julienned, plus 4
    sprigs for garnish

8 fresh chives, chopped

Mint-infused oil and sherry vinegar lend an elegance to this high-summer tomato salad, which is garnished with pine nuts, and snipped chives. Use the left-over mint oil to give a lift to barbecued lamb.

To prepare the mint oil, purée the mint leaves in a blender with the olive oil. Strain through a strainer lined with a cheesecloth into a small jar and set aside.

To prepare the vinaigrette, in a small bowl, whisk together the vinegar, lemon juice, shallot, and garlic, and let stand for 15 minutes. Slowly whisk in the olive oil. Season with salt and pepper and set aside.

Divide the tomato slices among 4 plates. Scatter the onion over the tomatoes and sprinkle with the pine nuts, julienned mint, and chives. Drizzle some of the mint oil and the vinaigrette on top, garnish with the mint sprigs, and serve.

Napkins

Napkins have always served a practical purpose, but they also go a long way in dressing up any table. In traditional settings, napkins are folded into rectangles or triangles, then placed to the left of the plate or on the charger. If informality is the order of the day, tradition can be set aside and the napkin placed wherever it looks best — in the center of the place, to the right of the soup spoon, or tucked in a glass.

A napkin can also be folded once, rolled up, tied in a knot, or shaken out, picked up in the center, and left on the table as it falls. At lunch, place cards or flowers can be tucked into napkin folds. For buffets or picnics, place settings of silverware can be individually wrapped in napkins and "served" in a basket, bowl, or decorative flower pot.

In the past, when for reasons of practicality napkins were reused, family members had initialed rings so they could identify their personal table linen. Today, napkin rings in a myriad of designs and materials are used mostly as table dressing and open other possibilities of personalizing each place setting. Antique silver ones give formal dinner tables a finished look. Less formal rings are made of silver, wood, plastic — or even ribbons, ivy, raffia, chive stems, silk cord, or little girls' bracelets.

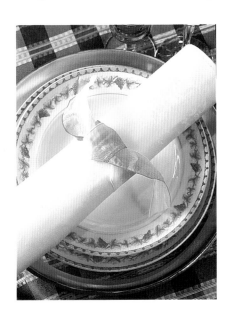

❖ CLEMENTINE, FENNEL, AND MOROCCAN OLIVE SALAD

SERVES 4

Vinaigrette:

Juice of 4 clementines (or 2 tangerines or 1 orange)

1 tablespoon minced onion or shallot

¹/₂ teaspoon ground toasted anise or fennel seeds

¹/₄ cup extra-virgin olive oil

Salad:

2 small fennel bulbs, thinly sliced

10 clementines (or 3 tangerines or 2 oranges), peeled and sectioned

24 Moroccan black olives, pitted

¹/₂ cup loosely packed mizuna leaves

1 tablespoon chopped fresh chives

Salt and freshly ground black pepper, to taste

1 tablespoon fennel seeds, toasted

Chef Matthew Kenney has made a name for himself by successfully adapting Moroccan cuisine for the American palate. His unusual salads attract a loyal following at his restaurant, Matthew's, in Manhattan. In this one, sweet fennel and tangy clementines are offset by pungent black olives. If they're out of season, the clementines can be replaced with oranges or tangerines.

To prepare the vinaigrette, in a small bowl, whisk together the clementine juice, onion, and anise. Slowly whisk in the olive oil. Set aside.

To prepare the salad, combine the fennel, clementines, olives, mizuna, and chives in a large salad bowl. Quickly whisk the vinaigrette, pour over the salad, and toss. Season with salt and pepper. Divide the salad among 4 plates, sprinkle with the fennel seeds, and serve.

Matthew's Meze Table

SPICED ALMONDS • SPICY RED CHUTNEY • MINT CHUTNEY

MIDDLE EASTERN SALSA VERDE • TAHINI YOGURT DIPPING SAUCE

FLATBREAD

LEMON VEGETABLE COUSCOUS (PAGE 124)

TOMATO, RED ONION, AND MINT SALAD (PAGE 50)

CLEMENTINE, FENNEL, AND MOROCCAN OLIVE SALAD

MOROCCAN SPICED CARROTS WITH
CUMIN-HONEY VINAIGRETTE (PAGE 119)

EGGPLANT SALAD WITH ALMONDS, DATES, AND MINT

HONEY-SWEETENED TEA • BEER • WINE

❖EGGPLANT SALAD WITH ALMONDS, DATES, AND MINT

SERVES 4

4 tablespoons olive oil

1 eggplant, cut into 1¹/₂-inch pieces

¹/₂ red onion, chopped

2 red bell peppers, cored, seeded, and cut into 1¹/₂-inch pieces

1 zucchini, cut into 1¹/₂-inch pieces

1 tablespoon balsamic vinegar

1 tablespoon tomato paste

1 tablespoon ground cumin

Pinch crushed red pepper flakes

Pinch sugar

Salt and freshly ground black pepper, to taste

¹/₃ cup sliced blanched almonds

¹/₄ cup pitted chopped fresh dates

1 teaspoon grated lemon zest

1 tablespoon chopped fresh mint, plus mint leaves for garnish

A trip to Morocco was the inspiration for Matthew Kenney's love affair with the flavors of North Africa: Fresh dates, almonds, dried fruits, and olives are at the heart of almost all his dishes. This salad combines eggplant with zucchini and bell peppers and is spiked with cumin, red pepper, and chopped mint. It can be served as part of a Moroccan meze table, a melange of salads, chutneys, and flatbreads.

Heat 1 tablespoon of the olive oil in a large nonstick skillet over medium-high heat. Sauté the eggplant, stirring occasionally, for 8 to 10 minutes, until well browned. Remove from the heat and set aside.

Heat 1 tablespoon of the olive oil in another large nonstick skillet over medium-high heat. Sauté the onion for 5 to 7 minutes, until translucent. Add the bell peppers and zucchini and cook, stirring occasionally, for 5 minutes. Add the eggplant, balsamic vinegar, tomato paste, cumin, red pepper flakes, sugar, salt, and pepper. Remove from the heat and let cool.

Heat the remaining 2 tablespoons olive oil in a skillet over medium heat. Sauté the almonds for 5 to 6 minutes, until golden brown. Add the dates and cook for about 4 minutes, until they begin to caramelize. Remove from the heat, let cool, and stir in the lemon zest.

In a large salad bowl, combine the vegetables, the almond mixture, and chopped mint. Toss, garnish with mint leaves, and serve.

❖ WEST STREET GRILL BEAN SALAD

SERVES 4 TO 6

¹/₄ cup extra-virgin olive oil

1 celery stalk, finely diced

¹/₂ red bell pepper, seeded and finely diced

1 red onion, finely diced

2 garlic cloves, minced

2 fresh sage sprigs

2 fresh thyme sprigs

2 bay leaves, preferably fresh

1 cup cooked flageolets

1 cup cooked yellow Steuben beans

1 cup cooked brown Swedish beans

1 cup cooked French navy beans

¹/₄ cup rice wine vinegar

2 plum tomatoes, diced

¹/₂ cup chopped fresh parsley

Freshly ground black pepper, to taste

Salt, to taste

Flageolets, yellow Steuben beans, brown Swedish beans, and French navy beans are included in this salad from the West Street Grill. If these varieties are not readily available, substitute a combination of dried beans such as black, kidney, pink, and lima beans.

Heat the olive oil in a large skillet over low heat. Add the celery, bell pepper, onion, and garlic and sauté for 5 minutes. Add the sage, thyme, and bay leaves and remove from the heat. Set aside for 10 minutes to allow the flavors to blend.

In a large serving bowl, combine all the beans and toss to mix well. Add the vegetable mixture and toss to combine. Set aside at room temperature for at least 1 hour. (The salad can be prepared to this point and refrigerated overnight. Bring to room temperature before continuing.)

In a small bowl, combine the vinegar, tomatoes, and parsley. Season with pepper. Add to the beans and toss to mix well. Taste to correct seasoning with salt and pepper, remove and discard the bay leaves, and serve.

❖ BLACK-EYED PEA SALSA

SERVES 6 TO 8

2 cups cooked black-eyed peas

¹/₂ red bell pepper, seeded and diced

¹/₂ red onion, finely chopped

1 small tomato, seeded and finely chopped

1 garlic clove, minced

2 tablespoons extra-virgin olive oil

2 tablespoons tomato juice

2 tablespoons red wine vinegar

2 tablespoons minced jalapeño chile pepper (wear rubber gloves when handling chile peppers)

1 tablespoon chopped fresh basil

1 tablespoon fresh lemon juice

¹/₂ teaspoon ground cumin

¹/₂ teaspoon chili powder

¹/₄ teaspoon salt

¹/₄ teaspoon freshly ground black pepper

This salsa is served as part of a hearty vegetarian platter at the Outermost Inn. To cook dried black-eyed peas, soak them overnight, drain, then simmer in fresh water to cover for 20 minutes, until they are tender. If you are short on time, canned black-eyed peas are a good short-cut.

In a large bowl, combine all the ingredients and toss to mix well. Cover and refrigerate for at least 30 minutes before serving.

❖ COUSCOUS SALAD

SERVES 4 TO 6

6 cups vegetable broth or water

¼ cup dried garlic flakes*

2 cups couscous

¼ cup extra-virgin olive oil

½ cup white wine vinegar

Salt and freshly ground black pepper, to taste

One 19-ounce can chick peas, rinsed and drained

1 cup dried currants

1 cup pine nuts, toasted

1 large cucumber, peeled, seeded, and chopped

2 green bell peppers, cored, seeded, and finely chopped

1 red onion, finely chopped

½ cup chopped fresh chives

1 cup chopped fresh flat-leaf parsley

Fresh lemon juice (optional)

*Dried garlic flakes are available in Asian and specialty food markets.

Leslie Hartnett cooks up a storm during the week to provide her customers at the Block Island Farmers' Market with good, ready-to-eat dishes, like this salad. A breeze to make, the quick-cooking couscous is combined with chick peas and fresh vegetables from the garden. This is a creative dish — add the summer vegetables you like.

Bring the broth to a boil in a large pot. Add the garlic flakes and slowly stir in the couscous. Remove from the heat and let sit for 5 minutes. Fluff gently with a fork.

Transfer the couscous to a large serving bowl. Sprinkle with the olive oil and vinegar and season with salt and pepper. Stir in the chick peas and fluff the couscous again with a fork. Allow to cool.

Add the currants, pine nuts, cucumber, bell peppers, onion, chives, and parsley and mix well. Sprinkle with lemon juice, if using, and serve.

❖ OLD-FASHIONED LENTIL SALAD

SERVES 4

1 ¹/₄ cups lentils

1 onion, halved

1 carrot, halved

2 shallots, 1 left whole and 1 minced

2 garlic cloves, smashed

1 bouquet garni of 1 bay leaf, 1 fresh parsley
    sprig, and 1 fresh thyme sprig, tied together
    with kitchen string

Salt, to taste

3¹/₂ ounces slab bacon, cubed

3 tablespoons white vinegar

6 tablespoons peanut oil

3 tablespoons white wine vinegar

1 teaspoon Dijon mustard

Freshly ground black pepper, to taste

Croutons, for garnish

Chopped fresh parsley, for garnish

*A Carrara marble dining table designed by her
husband is complemented by Jane Ellis's collection
of Wedgwood creamware, antique English cutlery,
wine rinsers, and silver and glass candlesticks.*

*From the Ritz-Escoffier cooking school in Paris, this French classic is
an ideal accompaniment to a country pâté or saucisson en croûte. It can also
be included in a buffet with a variety of other salads.*

Place the lentils in a large saucepan and add 8 cups cold water. Bring to a boil and skim the foam from the surface. Add the onion, carrot, whole shallot, the garlic, and bouquet garni, reduce the heat to low, and simmer for 30 minutes. Season with salt and cook for 5 minutes longer. Cover, set aside, and keep warm.

In a medium skillet, sauté the bacon over medium heat for about 6 minutes, until browned. Remove the bacon with a slotted spoon and set aside. Pour ¹/₄ cup of the bacon fat into a container and reserve. Add the white vinegar to the skillet, scrape up any browned bits, and simmer for 2 to 3 minutes, until slightly reduced. Set the pan aside.

Drain the lentils and discard the vegetables and bouquet garni. Place the lentils in a large serving bowl and cover. Set aside and keep warm.

In a small bowl, combine the bacon fat, the vinegar from the deglazed pan, the peanut oil, white wine vinegar, and mustard. Season with salt and pepper and mix well. Pour over the warm lentils, add the bacon and minced shallot, and toss to coat. Taste to correct the seasoning. Garnish with croutons and parsley and serve.

SERVING DISHES

If presentation is everything, the choice of serving platters is an important one. White, the favorite of chefs, is always safe, but patterned and colorful plates and bowls often enhance dishes. A glass plate set on top of a richly colored one lends added interest.

Unmatched pieces, antiques, or dishes intended for other purposes may be the perfect choice.

But there's more to a serving platter than a pretty face. It should be generous enough in size to accommodate the food, yet easy to handle.

❖ ROAST QUAIL AND CORN-FRIED OYSTER COBB SALAD

SERVES 6

Cornmeal batter:

½ cup cornmeal

¼ cup unbleached all-purpose flour

½ cup milk

1 large egg

¼ cup dark beer (or club soda)

Quail:

6 boneless quail

Salt and freshly ground black pepper, to taste

1 tablespoon olive oil

Oysters:

2 tablespoons vegetable oil

12 to 16 freshly shucked oysters

Salad:

6 tablespoons extra-virgin olive oil

2 tablespoons white wine vinegar

Salt and freshly ground black pepper, to taste

2 cups watercress leaves

1 pint pear or cherry tomatoes, halved

1 large avocado, pitted, peeled, and diced

3 slices bacon, cooked and crumbled

4 ounces Roquefort cheese, crumbled

Cobb Salad was invented in the 1920s by Bob Cobb of the Brown Derby restaurant in Los Angeles. Michael Lomonaco updated the recipe when he was chef at New York's "21" by replacing the chicken with quail and pan-fried oysters. Ask your butcher to bone the quail.

To prepare the batter, combine the cornmeal, flour, milk, egg, and beer in a stainless steel bowl. Do not overmix; small lumps will make the batter lighter. Refrigerate for at least 30 minutes.

To prepare the quail, preheat the oven to 350°F. Season the quail with salt and pepper. Heat the olive oil in a large heavy skillet over medium heat. Add the quail, breast-side down, and sauté until well browned, about 3 minutes. Turn and brown on the other side. Remove from the skillet and place in an ovenproof dish. Roast for 6 minutes, or until cooked through. Remove from the oven and set aside.

To prepare the oysters, heat the vegetable oil in a large heavy skillet over medium heat. With tongs, dip the oysters into the batter, then carefully lay them in the hot oil. Pan fry until golden brown, 1 to 2 minutes. Remove from the skillet and place on paper towels to drain.

To assemble the salad, in a small bowl, whisk together the olive oil and vinegar. Season with salt and pepper. In a large bowl, combine the watercress, tomatoes, avocado, bacon, and cheese. Quickly whisk the vinaigrette, pour over the salad, and toss. Transfer to a serving platter, top with the quail and oysters, and serve.

Fashion designer Geoffrey Beene likes a mix of patterns, textures, and colors for his table settings, just as in the clothes for which he is so famous. He loves contrasting geometrics, the punch of black and white with a burst of brilliant color, the plush feel of quilting. When he sets the table for company, he always tries to include some sort of reflecting surface such as silver, lacquer, mirrors, or glass — "anything that will give a double image" — to heighten the drama of the moment.

Beene's dining room is a menagerie of monochromatic prints. The walls and curtains carry a snow-leopard print, and the floors are carpeted in a zebra- and leopard-patterned wool. His black Karl Springer dining table is dressed with inexpensive spotted place mats from Indonesia that echo the black and white theme. White dinnerware edged in black completes the motif. Another nod to his asymmetrical style — one has only to think of his stunning bias-cut clothes — is a black lacquer compotier from Thailand, piled high with coconuts and a gold ball, and set off center. For an unexpected jolt of luscious color amid this celebration of black and white, the designer selected chartreuse wineglasses, striped tumblers — and orchids, his great passion.

3

THE MAIN COURSE

A dinner party is a gift, a tribute to family and friends. The food need not be elaborate, but it should reflect the style of the host and the occasion. Gone are the days when the measure of a great menu was how many days it took to prepare. When time is of the essence, a vast array of wonderful dishes can be made ahead (stews and daubes taste much better the next day) or prepared quickly once the ingredients are assembled.

Pasta is a favorite entrée for informal parties, and for good reason — immensely satisfying, it requires nothing more than some good bread, a glass of wine, and a salad afterward. And it is so versatile — the simple addition of caviar to angel hair pasta transforms it into a sublimely elegant dish. The sauces can often be made ahead of time and tossed with the pasta at the last minute.

Especially during colder weather, comfort food — meatloaf, shepherd's pie, chicken pot pie — never fails to please. This is the stuff of happy memories and second helpings.

An elegant roast, stuffed bird, or whole fish, presented with delectable side dishes of potatoes, vegetables, or rice, is perfect fare for a formal meal or any holiday.

Pasta

❖ PENNE WITH BROCCOLI RABE AND PINE NUTS

SERVES 4 TO 6

¹/₂ cup pine nuts, for garnish

1¹/₂ pounds broccoli rabe or other bitter greens, stems trimmed and rinsed

Salt, to taste

¹/₄ cup extra-virgin olive oil

4 or 5 garlic cloves, thinly sliced

Freshly ground black pepper, to taste

1 pound penne, macaroni, rigatoni or other pasta

¹/₄ cup freshly grated Pecorino Romano cheese

2 tablespoons unsalted butter, at room temperature (optional)

Tubular pastas are sturdy enough to stand up to chunky vegetable sauces. This simple combination of penne and broccoli rabe, from food writer Sally Schneider, makes a most satisfying dish.

Preheat the oven to 400°F. Spread the pine nuts in a single layer on a baking sheet and toast, stirring once or twice, for 5 to 7 minutes, until golden. Transfer the nuts to a plate and set aside.

Steam the broccoli rabe over ¹/₂ cup salted boiling water for about 5 minutes, until just tender. Remove and coarsely chop.

Heat the olive oil in a large skillet over medium heat. Reduce the heat to low, add the garlic, and cook for 5 to 6 minutes, until golden brown. Add the broccoli rabe and sauté for 2 to 3 minutes. Season with salt and pepper and remove the skillet from the heat.

Meanwhile, in a large pot of salted boiling water, cook the pasta according to the package instructions until al dente. Drain and transfer to a warm serving bowl. Add the broccoli rabe, cheese, and butter, if using, and toss to combine. Garnish with the pine nuts and serve.

❖ LINGUINE WITH OLIVE OIL AND CHIVES

SERVES 6

1 pound linguine

¹/₂ cup extra-virgin olive oil

Grated zest of 1 lemon

Juice of 2 lemons

³/₄ cup chopped fresh chives

¹/₄ cup chopped fresh parsley

Sea salt and freshly ground black pepper, to taste

6 chive flowers, for garnish (optional)

In summer, when fresh herbs are everywhere, use them to make lively pasta sauces for quick meals with close friends. This simple dish from the West Street Grill calls for a shower of freshly snipped chives, along with a little parsley, and a splash of olive oil.

In a large pot of salted boiling water, cook the pasta according to the package instructions until al dente. Drain and place in a large bowl.

Add the olive oil, lemon zest, lemon juice, chives, and parsley and toss to combine. Season with salt and pepper. Garnish with the chive flowers, if using, and serve immediately.

❖ SPAGHETTI WITH FRESH TOMATO SAUCE AND OLIVES

SERVES 4 TO 6

1 pound red and yellow tomatoes, seeded
    and diced (about 2 cups)

½ cup Kalamata olives, pitted and sliced

3 or 4 shallots, minced

2 tablespoons balsamic vinegar

⅓ cup chopped fresh basil

2 tablespoons mixed minced fresh herbs such
    as thyme, tarragon, cilantro, fennel tops,
    and/or flat-leaf parsley

Freshly ground black pepper, to taste

2 tablespoons extra-virgin olive oil

1 pound spaghetti, linguine, or bucatini

½ cup freshly grated Parmesan cheese,
    preferably Parmigiano-Reggiano

Coarsely ground black pepper, for serving

Nothing spells summer quite like a dish of pasta with a sauce made of garden-fresh tomatoes. This one calls for red and gold ones, as well as Kalamata olives, basil, vinegar, and oil. Serve it as a main course at lunch or a first course at dinner.

Combine the tomatoes, olives, shallots, vinegar, basil, mixed herbs, and pepper in a medium bowl. Drizzle with the olive oil and set aside.

In a large pot of salted boiling water, cook the pasta according to the package instructions until al dente. Drain and transfer to a warm serving bowl. Add the tomato mixture, toss to combine, and serve. Pass the Parmesan and coarsely ground pepper at the table.

❖ LEMON-SCENTED FETTUCCINE WITH SMOKED SALMON

SERVES 4

2 cups chicken broth

1 small fennel bulb, finely chopped, feathery
    tops reserved

1 onion, finely chopped

½ cup heavy cream

Salt and freshly ground black pepper, to taste

1 pound fettuccine

Grated zest and juice of 2 lemons, or to taste

12 ounces smoked salmon, julienned

Lemon and salmon, always natural companions, work well when combined with the slight sweetness of fennel purée in this refreshing, light pasta from chef Susan Weaver of Manhattan's Four Seasons Hotel.

In a saucepan over medium heat, combine the broth, chopped fennel, and onion. Bring to a simmer and cook for about 10 minutes, until the fennel is very tender. Add the cream and return to a simmer. Transfer to a blender and purée. Season with salt and pepper.

In a large pot of salted boiling water, cook the pasta according to the package instructions until al dente. Drain.

Meanwhile, transfer the fennel purée to a large skillet and bring to a simmer over medium heat. Reduce the heat to low.

Add the pasta, lemon zest and juice, and the smoked salmon to the sauce. Toss well and cook for 30 seconds. Transfer to a large warmed serving bowl, garnish with the reserved fennel tops, and serve.

❖ PASTA SHELLS WITH WILD MUSHROOM MEAT RAGU

SERVES 4 TO 6

2 ounces dried porcini mushrooms

2 tablespoons extra-virgin olive oil

1 tablespoon unsalted butter

2 carrots, finely chopped

1 large onion, finely chopped

2 garlic cloves, finely chopped

15 flat-leaf parsley sprigs, leaves only

1/2 pound boneless veal shoulder, lean beef, lamb, or game meat, cut into 1/4-inch dice

1/2 pound shiitake mushrooms, stemmed

1 cup dry red wine

Salt and freshly ground black pepper, to taste

1 1/2 pounds tomatoes, finely chopped, or one 28-ounce can Italian plum tomatoes, drained and finely chopped

1 cup homemade chicken broth (or low-sodium canned)

1 pound medium shell-shaped pasta, such as farfalle, fusilli, or orecchiette

1/2 cup green olives, pitted and sliced

Ragu — the quintessential pasta sauce — is best combined with pastas whose shapes will hold the meaty sauce: Farfalle, fusilli, and orecchiette are three good examples. Sally Schneider's veal ragu gets extra flavor from dried porcini and fresh shiitake mushrooms.

Soak the porcini in 2 1/2 cups lukewarm water for 30 minutes, or until soft. Remove the mushrooms with a slotted spoon and set aside.

Heat the olive oil and butter in a 2-quart flameproof casserole over medium heat. Sauté the carrots, onion, garlic, and parsley for 10 minutes, stirring frequently. Add the meat and cook, stirring frequently, for about 10 minutes until browned. Stir in the porcini and shiitake mushrooms and cook for 10 minutes more. Add the wine, stir, and continue to cook for 15 minutes. Season with salt and pepper.

Reduce the heat to low, add the tomatoes, and simmer, stirring frequently, for 30 minutes. Add 1/2 cup of the broth and cook, covered, for 15 minutes. Add the remaining 1/2 cup broth and cook, covered, for 15 minutes. Taste to correct the seasoning. Uncover and continue to cook for 10 to 15 minutes, until the sauce has thickened. (The sauce can be prepared to this point, covered, and set aside for up to 3 hours. Reheat before continuing.)

Meanwhile, in a large pot of salted boiling water, cook the pasta according to the package instructions until al dente. Drain.

Add the olives to the sauce and cook, uncovered, until heated through.

Transfer the pasta to a warm serving bowl. Add the sauce, toss to combine, and serve.

❖ SEMOLINA GNOCCHI WITH MEAT RAGU

SERVES 8 TO 10

Gnocchi:

5 1/2 cups milk

Large pinch ground saffron

3/4 pound very fine semolina flour

Freshly grated nutmeg, to taste

Salt and freshly ground black pepper, to taste

1/4 cup (1/2 stick) unsalted butter

1 extra-large egg

2 extra-large egg yolks

1/4 cup chicken broth, lukewarm

1/2 cup freshly grated Pecorino cheese

Ragu:

1/4 cup olive oil

3/4 cup (1 1/2 sticks) unsalted butter, cut into pats

1 pound boneless pork loin, in one piece, trimmed

3/4 pound boneless beef, in one piece, trimmed

1 cup dry red wine

1 red onion, chopped

2 garlic cloves

5 fresh basil leaves

2 pounds tomatoes, finely chopped, or one 28-ounce can Italian plum tomatoes, drained and passed through a food mill

Salt and freshly ground black pepper, to taste

1/2 cup freshly grated Pecorino cheese

In Italy, there are almost as many different kinds of gnocchi as there are pasta shapes. The dough can be made from potatoes, farina, cornmeal, bread crumbs, or flour. Here, the little dumplings, made with semolina flour, are layered with a meat sauce. Giuliano Bugialli demonstrates this recipe at his cooking classes, and it draws raves from his students. The gnocchi can be made a day in advance, as can the ragu.

To prepare the gnocchi, line a 15x10 1/2-inch jelly-roll pan with plastic wrap and lightly oil the plastic wrap. Rinse out a large saucepan with cold water. Add the milk and bring to a boil over medium heat. Add the saffron and begin adding the semolina very slowly, stirring constantly with a wooden spoon to prevent lumps from forming. When all the semolina has been incorporated, cook for 10 minutes, stirring constantly. Season with nutmeg, salt, and pepper. Add the butter and cook for 2 minutes more. Remove from the heat and stir for a few seconds.

Combine the egg, egg yolks, and broth in a bowl and add to the semolina. Stir in the cheese. Transfer to the prepared jelly-roll pan and spread out to an even thickness with a spatula moistened with hot water. Let the gnocchi cool for at least 1 hour. (The gnocchi can be prepared up to this point, covered, and refrigerated for up to 1 day.)

To prepare the ragu, heat the oil and 1/4 cup of the butter in a large saucepan over medium heat. Add the meats and cook, turning several times, for 10 minutes, until browned on all sides. Add the wine and cook for about 10 minutes, until the wine has evaporated. Remove from the heat. Cut the meat into thin strips and coarsely grind in a meat grinder. Return the meat to the pan, add the onion, and cook, stirring, over medium heat for 5 minutes.

Finely chop the garlic and basil together and add them to the casserole. Stir in the tomatoes and season with salt and pepper. Cook over low heat, covered, stirring occasionally, for 1 hour.

Preheat the oven to 375°F. Unmold the cooled gnocchi onto a large cutting board and cut it into 3-inch rounds with a biscuit cutter or the rim of a glass. Heavily coat a 9x13-inch glass baking dish with 2 tablespoons of the butter. Arrange half of the gnocchi rounds in one layer in the baking dish. Pour one third of the sauce over the top, sprinkle with half of the Pecorino, and dot with half of the remaining butter. Repeat the layering process and finish with a layer of sauce. Bake for 25 minutes, until heated through.

Let the gnocchi rest for about 5 minutes and serve.

❖ ANGEL HAIR PASTA WITH CAVIAR

SERVES 4

½ cup water

1 cup (2 sticks) butter, cut into small pieces

Salt and freshly ground white pepper, to taste

½ pound angel hair or capellini pasta

4 ounces sevruga caviar

When you want to splurge for a special celebration, it's hard to do better than this elegant dish from New York's March restaurant. Simply tossed with sweet butter, the pasta is crowned with a spoonful of caviar.

Bring the water to a boil in a large saucepan. Lower the heat and stir in the butter, a couple of pieces at a time, just until it is incorporated and the sauce thickens. Season with salt and pepper. Remove from the heat, cover, and keep warm.

Meanwhile, in a large pot of salted boiling water, cook the pasta according to the package instructions until al dente. Drain well.

Add the cooked pasta to the butter sauce and toss to coat. Divide the pasta among 4 bowls, top each with one quarter of the caviar, and serve immediately.

❖ ASPARAGUS RISOTTO

SERVES 6

4 cups water

2 vegetable bouillon cubes

2 garlic cloves, crushed

¼ cup extra-virgin olive oil

2 tablespoons finely chopped yellow onion

I pound fresh asparagus, tips cut off and reserved, stalks sliced into ½-inch pieces

1½ cups Arborio rice

I cup dry white wine

¼ cup freshly grated Parmesan cheese

½ cup chopped fresh flat-leaf parsley

French-born potter Martine Vermeulen almost always serves a pasta or risotto to guests for lunch or dinner. For this risotto (a creamy union of Italian short-grain rice, broth and Parmesan), the asparagus is cooked briefly and combined with the rice only at the last minute to keep it crisp and tasty.

In a saucepan over medium heat, bring the water, bouillon cubes, and 1 of the garlic cloves to a simmer.

Meanwhile, heat the olive oil in a large heavy saucepan over medium-high heat, Sauté the onion and the remaining garlic clove for 3 to 4 minutes, until the onion is translucent. Add the asparagus tips and cook, stirring constantly, for about 1 minute. Remove the tips with a slotted spoon and set aside. Add the asparagus stalks to the pan and cook, stirring constantly, for about 2 minutes. Remove the stalks and set aside. Add the rice to the pan and sauté, stirring to coat with the oil, for 2 minutes.

Add ½ cup of the wine and cook, stirring, until the liquid is absorbed. Add the remaining ½ cup wine and cook, stirring, until the liquid is absorbed. Continue adding broth ½ cup at a time and stirring until the liquid is absorbed. The risotto is done when it is creamy but still tender to the bite. This should take 20 to 30 minutes.

Spoon the risotto into a warm serving bowl and toss with the asparagus stalks. Garnish with the asparagus tips, Parmesan, and parsley, and serve.

❖RISOTTO PESTO PRIMAVERA

SERVES 6

Pesto:

6 tablespoons chopped fresh basil

3 tablespoons chopped fresh flat-leaf parsley

2 tablespoons freshly grated Parmesan cheese

2 tablespoons olive oil

I tablespoon toasted pine nuts

I tablespoon chopped walnuts

I garlic clove, minced

Vegetables:

¹/₄ cup diced zucchini

¹/₄ cup peas

¹/₄ cup chopped broccoli

¹/₄ cup chopped asparagus

Risotto:

4 to 5 cups chicken broth, preferably
   homemade

2 tablespoons olive oil

I small white onion, chopped

1¹/₂ cups Arborio rice

¹/₄ cup dry white wine

I teaspoon salt, or to taste

I tablespoon butter

I tablespoon freshly grated Parmesan cheese

A fragrant pesto sauce and a variety of spring vegetables, including peas, broccoli, and zucchini, give this risotto its bright green hue. It comes from chef Francesco Antonucci of Remi in New York. His secret for perfection: The risotto should be finished — cooked and creamy — in about twenty minutes of close attention, and then served immediately.

To prepare the pesto, in a food processor, combine the basil, parsley, Parmesan, olive oil, pine nuts, walnuts, and garlic. Process to a coarse purée. Transfer to a small bowl and set aside.

To prepare the vegetables, in a vegetable steamer over boiling water, steam the zucchini, peas, broccoli, and asparagus for about 5 minutes, until just tender. Set aside.

To prepare the risotto, bring the broth to a simmer in a medium saucepan over medium heat.

Heat the olive oil in a large heavy saucepan over low heat. Sauté the onion for about 3 minutes, until translucent. Add the rice and sauté, stirring to coat with the oil, for 2 minutes.

Add the wine and cook, stirring, until the liquid is absorbed. Add 1 cup of the broth and cook, stirring, until the liquid is absorbed. Continue adding broth ¹/₂ cup at a time and stirring until the liquid is absorbed. The risotto is done when it is creamy but still tender to the bite. This should take 18 to 20 minutes.

Add the vegetables and pesto to the risotto and stir to combine well. Cook, stirring, until the vegetables are heated through. Season with the salt. Remove the risotto from the heat and stir in the butter and Parmesan. Serve.

Table Settings

At Barbara Wirth's informal pink and green party table (opposite), the centerpiece is a luscious spill of golden grapes surrounded by a scattering of bud vases holding roses. There are more flowers hand-painted on the canvas chair backs to make a setting for dinner that has the appeal of a beautiful garden. In the winter months, Wirth prefers a color scheme of fire engine red and cobalt blue (above).

Setting the table for a party can be just as creative and personal as devising the menu and preparing the food. Whether we use treasured china and linens or improvise with mixed pieces and found objects, it is an opportunity to reflect our mood and taste. "It's like dressing yourself," says designer Bunny Williams. "You don't want to wear the same outfit every day. You want the fun of change."

The table itself can be left bare, with just the warmth of the wood to make the silver sparkle. Or it can be covered with a cloth: snowy linen or damask, lengths of batik, upholstery fabric, antique bed covers, quilts, or checked gingham — the choices are rich and varied. Napkins, from family heirlooms and linen hand towels or tea towels to flea market finds, should be generous in size and perfectly pristine but need not match either the tablecloth or each other.

Happily, even the most formal dinner party no longer requires one's best wedding porcelain. Artfully mixing different patterns of china, pottery, glassware, and flatware, or combining family heirlooms with thrift store pieces can result in a unique and appealing table. Adding unmatched pieces to an existing collection is a simple matter of staying within a color palette and style that complements the room — be it a formal dining room, kitchen, or patio.

A sparkling column of crystal goblets and pitchers lights up the holiday table (opposite). Touches of color come from red-patterned dessert plates and the flowers.

Eight different place settings in a matchless mix of patterns (two details in the photographs below) and a green, white, gold, and berry palette are used for the table setting (bottom). The serendipitous effect proves that an elegant mix and clever layering works for the table just as it does for a wardrobe.

*Seafood*

❖ CURRIED SALMON EN PAPILLOTE

SERVES 4

2 zucchini, julienned

2 carrots, julienned

$\frac{1}{2}$ cup (1 stick) unsweetened butter

4 small white onions, thinly sliced

2 tablespoons curry powder

2 cups dry white wine

Four 6-ounce skinless salmon fillets

Salt and freshly ground black pepper, to taste

$\frac{1}{2}$ cup peas

6 to 8 plum tomatoes, seeded and cut into strips

8 sprigs fresh flat-leaf parsley

Cooking fish in parchment paper — en papillote — allows it to steam in its own juices. It looks spectacular, too, as the parchment paper puffs up into an attractive dome. Here, the salmon is steamed with vegetables and curried butter; it's a specialty of New York's Cub Room.

In a large pot of salted boiling water, blanch the zucchini for 30 seconds. Remove with a slotted spoon and drain in a colander. Cook the carrots in the boiling water for 4 to 5 minutes, until al dente. Refresh in cold water and drain.

Preheat the oven to 450°F. Melt $\frac{1}{4}$ cup of the butter in a small skillet over medium heat. Sauté the onions with the curry powder for 6 to 8 minutes, until the onions are translucent. Add the wine, raise the heat to high, and boil to reduce the liquid to 1 cup. Slowly add the remaining $\frac{1}{4}$ cup butter, in small pieces, whisking constantly until the butter is absorbed. Set aside.

Fold four 24-inch-square pieces of parchment paper (or aluminum foil) in half and lightly butter one side of each. Place the salmon fillets on one side of each sheet and season with salt and pepper. Top the salmon with the zucchini, carrots, peas, tomatoes, parsley, and the onion mixture. Fold the parchment over the salmon and vegetables and seal tightly on all sides with small pleats. Place the packets on a large rimmed baking sheet and bake for about 10 to 12 minutes, until the packets inflate. Transfer the packets to dinner plates, cut them open, and serve immediately.

❖ CRISP ROASTED SALMON WITH CITRUS SAUCE

SERVES 8 TO 10

One 3½- to 4-pound salmon fillet, skin on, at
    room temperature
Sea salt and freshly ground black pepper,
    to taste
Extra-virgin olive oil
½ bunch fresh dill, finely chopped
4 shallots, finely diced
12 fresh thyme sprigs
6 fresh rosemary sprigs
½ cup dry vermouth
Citrus Sauce (recipe follows)

Salmon, roasted under the broiler to crisply char the skin, is served here with a tangy sauce made from oranges, lemons, and limes. Artist Thomas McKnight and his wife, Renate, often serve this dish at parties.

Preheat the broiler. Sprinkle the flesh side of the salmon with salt and pepper and rub with olive oil. Place the dill, shallots, thyme, and rosemary in a shallow roasting pan. Place the salmon on top of the herbs, skin-side up, and pour the vermouth around the salmon. Broil the salmon 6 inches from the heat for 12 to 15 minutes, until the skin is charred and crisp. Transfer to a serving platter, slice, and serve with the Citrus Sauce on the side.

CITRUS SAUCE

MAKES ABOUT 1½ CUPS

Juice of 6 oranges
Juice of 2 lemons
Juice of 2 limes
Salt and freshly ground black pepper, to taste

Combine the juices in a small saucepan over medium-high heat. Simmer until reduced by half. Season with salt and pepper.

Buffet for a Crowd

CROSTINI WITH FOUR TOPPINGS (PAGE 4)
DEVILLED EGGS

PORK ROASTED IN BEER (PAGE 107)
CRISP ROASTED SALMON WITH CITRUS SAUCE

PICKLED BEETS • ARTICHOKE HEARTS
SHALLOTS IN RED WINE (PAGE 123)
STUFFED PEPPERS

BEER • SELTZER
CHARDONNAY
CHOCOLATE TART (PAGE 151)
POACHED PEARS WITH BRANDY AND GINGER (PAGE 136)

❖ GRILLED SHRIMP AND VEGETABLES

SERVES 6

Shrimp:

1 cup olive oil

¼ cup brandy

3 garlic cloves, minced

1 lemon, thinly sliced

Salt and freshly ground black pepper, to taste

2 pounds large shrimp, shells on

Vegetables:

½ cup olive oil

Juice of ½ lemon

Salt and freshly ground black pepper, to taste

1 pound mushrooms, stems trimmed

1 pound cherry or plum tomatoes, halved

1 bunch arugula

2 tablespoons extra-virgin olive oil

1 tablespoon balsamic vinegar

Lemon wedges

Salt and freshly ground black pepper, to taste

These nicely browned vegetables and succulent shrimp are delicious on a bed of arugula (watercress or a mix of baby greens are good substitutes). For stress-free barbecuing, the shrimp and vegetables can be marinated and skewered long before guests arrive.

To marinate the shrimp, in a shallow dish, combine the olive oil, brandy, garlic, lemon, salt, and pepper. Add the shrimp and toss to coat. Cover with plastic wrap and refrigerate for at least 1 hour, or overnight.

To marinate the vegetables, in a medium bowl, combine the olive oil, lemon juice, salt, and pepper. Add the mushrooms and tomatoes and toss to coat. Cover with plastic wrap and set aside at room temperature for at least 1 hour.

Preheat the grill to medium-hot and brush with oil. Skewer the shrimp, mushrooms, and tomatoes separately on 10 to 12 skewers. Place the mushrooms on the grill and cook for 4 minutes, then add the shrimp and tomatoes and grill, turning once, for about 10 minutes, until the vegetables and shrimp are nicely browned.

Meanwhile, in a medium bowl, toss the arugula with the olive oil and vinegar. Place a small bed of arugula on each of 6 plates. Place the shrimp, tomatoes, and mushrooms on top of the arugula. Add a squeeze of lemon, season with salt and pepper, and serve.

FLAVORFUL GRILLING

Herb branches, spice sticks, sugarcane slivers, and lemongrass add style and taste to grilled foods that metal or even wooden skewers simply cannot. Cookbook author Steven Raichlen suggests threading marinated shrimp on sugarcane, then brushing with a rum glaze as they grill. Vegetables take on a lemony flavor when grilled on lemongrass. A thin slice of star fruit grilled on a cinnamon stick makes a low-calorie lollipop. Rosemary branches impart their woodsy flavor to chicken or lamb kabobs.

❖ NEW ENGLAND SEAFOOD CHOWDER

SERVES 8

2 pounds skinless white fish fillets (such as bass, cod, or haddock), cut into 2-inch pieces

2 cups fish broth

½ cup (1 stick) butter

½ onion, chopped

1 celery stalk, chopped

½ cup all-purpose flour

½ pound red potatoes, cut into ½-inch cubes

2 tablespoons chopped fresh parsley, plus more for garnish

1 bay leaf

1 pound sea scallops, coarsely chopped

1 pound shrimp, peeled, deveined, and coarsely chopped

½ pound cooked fresh lobster meat

3 cups half-and-half

Salt and freshly ground black pepper, to taste

Scallops, shrimp, lobster, fish fillets, and potatoes make for a delightfully chunky soup in the rich and creamy New England tradition.

In a large heavy pot over medium heat, combine the fish and broth and bring to a boil. Cover, reduce the heat, and simmer for 4 to 5 minutes. Drain the fish, reserving the broth, and set aside.

Melt the butter in a large heavy pot over medium heat. Sauté the onion and celery for 4 to 5 minutes, until tender. Add the flour and cook, stirring, for 4 minutes. Add the reserved fish broth and mix well. Add the potatoes, parsley, and bay leaf and simmer for 8 to 10 minutes, until the potatoes are tender. Add the scallops and shrimp and simmer for 2 to 3 minutes, until firm. Add the lobster meat and cooked fish and stir well.

Meanwhile, heat the half-and-half over medium heat until hot and add to the seafood mixture. Cook the chowder, stirring frequently, until slightly thickened and smooth, about 3 minutes. Season with salt and pepper. Remove and discard the bay leaf. Ladle the chowder into soup bowls, garnish with parsley, and serve.

❖ SPICY CRAB CAKES

SERVES 8

Spicy olive oil:

1 teaspoon ground cumin

1 teaspoon coriander seeds

1 teaspoon ground ginger

$\frac{1}{2}$ teaspoon ground cinnamon

$\frac{1}{2}$ teaspoon crushed red pepper flakes

3 star anise

Salt, to taste

2 cups extra-virgin olive oil

Tomatoes:

1 teaspoon olive oil

1 shallot, finely diced

6 tomatoes, peeled, seeded, and diced

1 tablespoon tomato paste

2 fresh thyme sprigs

1 bay leaf

Salt and freshly ground black pepper, to taste

Crab cakes:

1 pound fresh lump crabmeat, picked over
   for shells

1 bunch fresh cilantro, finely chopped

4 shallots, finely diced

1 jalapeño chile pepper, stemmed, seeded, and
   finely diced (wear rubber gloves when
   handling chile peppers)

3 tablespoons mayonnaise

1 tablespoon olive oil

Fresh basil sprigs, for garnish

At the 1939 World's Fair, traditional Southern crab cakes became a national favorite, and they have been at the top of the popularity charts ever since. Claude Troisgros gives them a Brazilian zing with the addition of jalapeños.

To prepare the spicy olive oil, mix together all the spices in a medium saucepan. Add the olive oil and heat over medium heat until the oil is hot. Remove from the heat and allow to cool. Pour into a clean glass bottle, seal, and refrigerate until ready to use. (The oil can be prepared ahead and refrigerated for up to 2 weeks. The longer the oil sits, the more flavorful it will become.)

To prepare the tomatoes, heat the olive oil in a heavy saucepan over medium heat. Sauté the shallot for about 3 minutes, until soft. Add the tomatoes, tomato paste, thyme, bay leaf, salt, and pepper and cook, stirring occasionally, until the mixture has broken down and is reduced by half, about 30 minutes. Remove from the heat and set aside to cool. Remove and discard the bay leaf and thyme. (The tomatoes can be prepared ahead, covered, and refrigerated for up to 2 days. Bring to room temperature before continuing.)

To prepare the crab cakes, in a bowl, mix together the crabmeat, cilantro, shallots, jalapeño, and mayonnaise until well combined.

Place eight 3x2$\frac{1}{2}$-inch ring molds on a parchment-lined baking sheet. Spread 2 tablespoons of the crab mixture evenly in the bottom of each ring mold. Top with 2 tablespoons of the tomato mixture, then continue with another layer of crab and a final layer of tomato. Refrigerate until ready to cook.

Preheat the oven to 400°F. Heat the olive oil in a large heavy ovenproof skillet over medium-high heat. With a spatula, carefully place the ring molds in the skillet, crab-side down, and sauté for about 3 minutes, until the bottoms are golden brown. Transfer the skillet to the oven and bake for 15 minutes. Allow the molds to cool in the skillet for 2 minutes. With a spatula, carefully remove the crab cakes from the skillet and invert onto a serving plate, crab-side up. Gently remove the molds with an oven mitt. Drizzle 1 to 2 tablespoons of the spicy olive oil around the crab cakes, garnish with basil sprigs, and serve.

❖ SEAFOOD POT PIE WITH TARRAGON BISCUITS

SERVES 4 TO 6

Biscuits:

2 cups all-purpose flour

2 teaspoons baking powder

1 ½ teaspoons baking soda

1 ½ teaspoons salt

1 cup buttermilk

3 tablespoons chopped fresh tarragon

¼ cup (½ stick) very cold unsalted butter, cut into walnut-size pieces

Seafood:

2 tablespoons unsalted butter

12 large shrimp (about ½ pound), peeled, deveined, and butterflied

Salt and freshly ground black pepper, to taste

1 pound red snapper fillets, skin on, cut into 2-inch pieces

2 leeks, white and light green parts, diced and well washed

2 large carrots, finely diced

3 large shallots, finely diced

1 teaspoon saffron threads

¼ cup dry white wine

1 ½ cups fish broth (or canned low-sodium chicken or vegetable broth)

¼ cup heavy cream

3 tablespoons chopped fresh tarragon, plus whole leaves for garnish

This light update of classic pot pie comes from Michael Lomonaco, who substitutes shrimp and red snapper for the traditional chicken. A few tarragon biscuits take the place of a heavy crust.

To prepare the biscuits, sift together the flour, baking powder, baking soda, and salt into a large bowl. In a small bowl, combine the buttermilk and tarragon. Beating with an electric mixer set on the lowest speed, slowly add the buttermilk to the dry ingredients. Beat in the butter; do not overbeat — allow the mixture to remain lumpy in texture (this will help give the biscuits a flaky texture). Cover and refrigerate for 20 minutes.

Preheat the oven to 350°F. Turn the dough out onto a lightly floured surface. With the palm of your hand, pat the dough into a square about 1½ inches thick. With a small biscuit cutter, cut into rounds (you should have about 24 biscuits). Place the biscuits on a nonstick baking sheet and bake for 12 minutes, until golden brown.

To prepare the seafood, melt 1 tablespoon of the butter in a large skillet over high heat. Add the shrimp, season with salt and pepper, and cook, turning once, for 4 minutes, until lightly browned. With a slotted spoon, transfer the shrimp to a bowl. Add the red snapper to the skillet, skin-side up, season with salt and pepper, and cook for 2 minutes. Turn the snapper over and cook for 2 to 3 minutes more, until the skin is crisp. With a slotted spoon, transfer the snapper to the bowl with the shrimp.

Add the remaining 1 tablespoon butter to the skillet and heat over medium heat until it begins to foam. Sauté the leeks, carrots, and shallots for 2 minutes. Add the saffron and cook for 1 minute more. Add the wine and cook for 2 minutes. Raise the heat to high, add the broth, and bring to a boil. Reduce the heat to low and simmer for about 5 minutes. Return the shrimp and snapper to the skillet and gently simmer for 5 minutes. Add the cream and cook for 1 minute more, until heated through. Stir in the chopped tarragon.

Divide the seafood and broth among individual soup bowls. Top with the biscuits, garnish with tarragon leaves, and serve.

❖ ATLANTIC FISH RAGOUT WITH SAFFRON MAYONNAISE

SERVES 8 TO 10

Fish stock:

6 tablespoons olive oil

1 onion, finely diced

2 leeks, finely diced and well washed

5 celery stalks, finely diced

1 fennel bulb, thinly sliced

1/2 cup chopped fresh flat-leaf parsley

1 garlic head, cloves separated and thinly sliced

3 pounds fish heads and bones (from any nonoily white fish), gills removed and rinsed well

4 tomatoes, peeled, seeded, and chopped

1/2 cup tomato puree

2 bay leaves

3 quarts water

Pinch saffron threads

Salt and freshly ground black pepper, to taste

Ragout:

1 onion, thinly sliced

1 fennel bulb, thinly sliced

4 tomatoes, peeled, seeded, and coarsely chopped

1 leek, thinly sliced and well washed

2 1/2 pounds potatoes, peeled and cubed

1 pound red snapper fillets, cut into 2-inch pieces

1 pound black bass fillets, cut into 2-inch pieces

1 pound halibut steaks, cut into 2-inch pieces

1 pound cod fillets, cut into 2-inch pieces

1 pound mussels, scrubbed and debearded

1 dozen littleneck clams, scrubbed

1/2 pound medium shrimp, peeled and deveined

3 lobster tails and 6 claws, in the shell, cut into 1-inch pieces (optional)

Saffron mayonnaise and croutons:

1/4 teaspoon powdered saffron

1 cup mayonnaise

Ground red pepper, to taste

1/4 cup olive oil

1 teaspoon garlic purée

1 baguette (about 8 inches long), sliced

A variation on bouillabaisse, this ragout is made from cold-water fish — halibut, black bass, and red snapper — along with shrimp, mussels, and clams. Chef Henry Meer adds a saffron-flavored mayonnaise, spread on garlic-scented toast.

To prepare the stock, heat the olive oil in a large heavy pot over medium-high heat. Sauté the onion, leeks, celery, fennel, parsley, and garlic for 10 to 12 minutes, until the onions are translucent. Add the fish heads and bones, tomatoes, tomato purée, and bay leaves, and cook, stirring constantly, for about 5 minutes, until the fish bones are opaque.

Add the water to the pot and bring to a boil. Reduce the heat to medium and simmer for 30 minutes, skimming off any foam that rises to the top. Strain the stock through cheesecloth set in a fine-mesh strainer into a large bowl. Discard the solids and strain again.

Pour the stock into a clean pot, bring to a simmer over medium heat, and reduce to about 8 cups. Add the saffron and continue to simmer for 5 minutes more. Season with salt and pepper and set aside. (The stock can be prepared ahead and refrigerated for 2 to 3 days.)

To prepare the ragout, in a large pot over medium heat, bring the fish stock to a simmer. Add the onion, fennel, tomatoes, leek, and potatoes. Simmer, partially covered, for 10 minutes. Add the snapper, bass, halibut, cod, mussels, clams, shrimp, and the lobster, if using, and gently simmer, covered, for 5 to 10 minutes, until the fish and seafood are cooked through.

Meanwhile, to prepare the saffron mayonnaise, dissolve the saffron in 1 tablespoon of the hot fish soup. In a small bowl, mix together the mayonnaise, saffron mixture, and red pepper.

To prepare the croutons, preheat the oven to 375°F. Combine the olive oil and garlic purée. Brush one side of each slice of bread with the mixture. Place on a baking sheet and bake for about 10 minutes, until lightly browned. Let cool to room temperature.

To serve, spread about 1 1/2 teaspoons of the mayonnaise on each crouton. Divide the seafood among heated soup bowls and ladle the broth over the top. Garnish with the croutons and serve. Pass the remaining mayonnaise at the table.

❖ CURRIED BREAST OF CHICKEN ON RICE SALAD

SERVES 6

Rice salad:

3½ cups water

1 lemon, thinly sliced

One 1-inch piece fresh ginger, peeled

1 garlic clove

1 fresh mint sprig

Salt, to taste

1 tablespoon olive oil

2 cups basmati rice

2 tablespoons rice vinegar mixed with 2
    teaspoons sugar

Curried chicken:

¼ cup olive oil

1½ tablespoons curry powder

6 skinless boneless chicken breast halves

¼ cup white wine or chicken broth

Salt, to taste

Fruit chutney, pine nuts, currants plumped in
    a little white wine, avocado cubes tossed
    with lime juice, sour cream or yogurt, lime
    wedges, and/or cilantro sprigs, for garnish

This perfect cook-ahead dish, served at room temperature, combines the pungent zing of curry with an array of sweet and rich garnishes; serve them all and let your guests choose.

To prepare the rice salad, preheat the oven to 350°F. In a large flameproof casserole over low heat, combine the water, lemon, ginger, garlic, mint, and salt and bring to a simmer.

Meanwhile, heat the olive oil in a large skillet over medium heat. Sauté the rice, stirring, for 2 minutes. Stir the rice into the simmering water, cover, and bake for 15 minutes, until tender. Remove and discard the ginger, garlic, and mint sprig and fluff the rice with a fork. Drizzle the vinegar mixture over the rice, fluff again, and set aside to cool completely.

To prepare the chicken, reduce the oven temperature to 325°F. Combine the olive oil and curry powder in a large heavy skillet over medium heat and cook for 2 minutes, stirring constantly. Reduce the heat to low, add the chicken, and cook, turning once, for 5 to 6 minutes, until lightly browned. Transfer the chicken to a large baking dish and set aside.

Add the wine to the skillet and cook, scraping up any browned bits, until reduced slightly. Pour over the chicken, season with salt, and cover the dish tightly with aluminum foil. Bake for 15 minutes, or until the chicken is cooked through. Loosen the foil and cool to room temperature.

Slice the chicken on the diagonal into thick slices. Divide the rice among 6 dinner plates. Top each portion with a sliced chicken breast and 2 tablespoons of the pan juices. Serve with a selection of garnishes.

❖ ROASTED CHICKEN

SERVES 8

2 small chickens (about 2½ pounds each),
    quartered

1½ cups water or 1 cup water and ½ cup
    white wine

One 5-ounce bottle Worcestershire sauce

Juice of 3 lemons

Chopped fresh parsley, for garnish

The secret ingredient in John Rosselli's roasted chicken is Worcestershire sauce — a whole bottle of it. Combined with lemon juice and water, it makes a quick and tasty basting sauce. This is hassle-free party food at its best.

Preheat the oven to 350°F. Place the chicken, skin-side up, in a shallow roasting pan. Mix together the water, Worcestershire, and lemon juice in a bowl and pour over the chicken pieces.

Roast the chicken, basting every 15 minutes with the pan juices, for about 1 hour, until cooked through. (Do not turn the chicken during roasting.) Transfer the chicken to a warm serving platter.

Place the roasting pan over medium-high heat and cook, scraping up any browned bits, until the pan juices are reduced by half. Pour the sauce into a heated sauceboat. Garnish the chicken with the parsley and serve, passing the sauce at the table.

❖ CHICKEN WITH PANCETTA, POTATOES, AND BLACK OLIVES

SERVES 4

1 thick slice pancetta or smoked bacon
    (about 2 ounces), cubed

1 tablespoon peanut oil

1 tablespoon olive oil

1 large onion, quartered and cut crosswise
    into ½-inch slices

1 chicken (about 4 pounds), cut into 8 pieces

1 teaspoon sweet paprika

Salt and freshly ground black pepper, to taste

About 2 cups chicken broth

6 red potatoes (about 1½ pounds),
    peeled and cut in half

8 black olives, pitted

2 tablespoons minced fresh flat-leaf parsley

Pancetta (an Italian cured bacon) and earthy black olives lend their full flavor to this quick fricassee. If you can't find pancetta, try it with smoked bacon — the dish will not be quite the same, but delicious nonetheless.

In a small saucepan over medium-high heat, combine the pancetta and enough cold water to cover. Simmer for 10 minutes. Drain and rinse under cold water.

Heat a large skillet over medium heat. Cook the pancetta for 2 minutes, until lightly browned. Add the peanut and olive oils and heat until hot but not smoking. Stir in the onion and cook for about 5 minutes, until lightly browned. Add the chicken pieces, skin-side down, and cook, turning once, for about 12 minutes, until browned. Sprinkle with the paprika and season with salt and pepper.

Add just enough broth to barely cover the chicken. Raise the heat to high and bring to a boil. Add the potatoes, reduce the heat to low, cover, and simmer for 15 minutes, until the chicken is cooked through. Transfer the chicken to a bowl and keep warm.

Cook the potatoes for 5 to 10 minutes more, until tender. Return the chicken to the skillet and heat through. Stir in the olives. Taste to correct seasoning, garnish with parsley, and serve.

❖ BASQUE CHICKEN

SERVES 4

2 green bell peppers

1 red bell pepper

¹/₃ cup olive oil

2 large onions, sliced

1 cup canned tomatoes with their juice, chopped

4 garlic cloves, minced

Salt and freshly ground black pepper, to taste

1 chicken (about 4 pounds), quartered

Bell peppers are grown in abundance in Basque country, so anything labeled "Basque" is sure to have at least one or two peppers in the ingredients. These chicken pieces also gain flavor from garlic, onions, and tomatoes. The recipe is from the Ritz-Escoffier cooking school in Paris.

Roast the bell peppers over a gas or charcoal flame, or under a broiler, turning occasionally, for 15 minutes, or until blackened on all sides. Transfer to a plastic bag, seal tightly, and steam for 10 minutes. When cool enough to handle, peel, core, and seed the peppers. Cut into thin strips and set aside.

Heat 3 tablespoons of the olive oil in a large skillet over medium heat. Sauté the onions for 5 to 6 minutes, until translucent. Add the pepper strips, tomatoes and their juice, and the garlic. Season with salt and pepper. Stir to mix thoroughly and set aside.

Season the chicken with salt and pepper. Heat the remaining olive oil in a large skillet over medium-high heat. Add the chicken and cook, turning, until browned, about 10 minutes. Remove the chicken from the pan and discard fat. Add the onion-pepper mixture to the pan and place the chicken on top. Cover, reduce the heat to medium, and cook, turning the chicken once, for 25 to 30 minutes, until cooked through.

Spoon the onion-pepper mixture onto a warm platter, place the chicken on top, and serve.

❖ POACHED ROULADE OF CHICKEN

SERVES 6

6 large skinless boneless chicken breast halves

2 tablespoons olive oil

3 garlic cloves minced

1 shallot, minced

10 ounces spinach, stems trimmed and well washed (about 6 cups)

4 ounces sun-dried tomatoes packed in oil, roughly diced

8 ounces chèvre (goat cheese) or sheep's milk cheese

1/4 cup pine nuts, toasted

2 large egg whites, lightly beaten

3 tablespoons plain dried bread crumbs

Salt and freshly ground black pepper, to taste

These spinachy chicken rolls are delicious on a bed of baby field greens tossed with your favorite vinaigrette. With lime-spiced fresh corn, they make a nice luncheon entree. Or you could slice the roulades thinly and serve them as hors d'oeuvres.

Place the chicken between pieces of plastic wrap and pound with a meat pounder until they are a uniform thickness. Refrigerate until ready to use.

Heat the olive oil in a large skillet over medium heat. Sauté the garlic and shallot for 2 minutes, until softened. Add the spinach and cook for about 2 minutes, until wilted. Stir in the sun-dried tomatoes and cook for 1 minute more. Remove from the heat and allow to cool.

Squeeze the spinach mixture to release excess liquid, roughly chop, and place in a bowl. Fold in the cheese, pine nuts, and egg whites. Add the bread crumbs, season with salt and pepper, and combine well.

Fill a pastry bag fitted with a large plain tip with the spinach mixture. Place 1 piece of chicken, skinned-side down, on a 12x8-inch piece of plastic wrap. Pipe a band of stuffing lengthwise down the chicken. Fold in the short sides of the chicken and roll it up lengthwise. Wrap the roulade in the plastic wrap, twist the ends tightly, and knot. Repeat with the remaining chicken and stuffing.

In a large pot of boiling water, poach the roulades for about 30 minutes, until the inside of chicken reaches 145°F on an instant-read thermometer. Remove the roulades from the liquid and allow to cool slightly. Carefully remove the plastic wrap, slice each roulade crosswise into 4 equal pieces, and serve.

❖ CHICKEN POT PIE

SERVES 4

1 piece frozen puff pastry (about ½ pound), thawed

2 pounds skinless boneless chicken breasts and thighs

1 bay leaf

4 or 5 peppercorns

3 tablespoons butter

2 tablespoons all-purpose flour

1 cup heavy cream

½ teaspoon Tabasco sauce

Salt and freshly ground black pepper, to taste

1½ cups tiny pearl onions, peeled

1 cup fresh or frozen small peas

1 large egg, beaten

A classic American dish, chicken pot pie is true comfort food. The filling can be prepared up to two days ahead and refrigerated. However, the frozen puff pastry should be added just before baking. The secret to the puffy crust of this pot pie is to make sure that everything is cold when it goes in the oven says its creator, House Beautiful's Mary Ellen Weinrib.

To prepare the crust, line a baking sheet with waxed paper. Place a plastic chopping board in the freezer for 5 minutes.

Lightly flour the chopping board and roll out the puff pastry to cover the top of a 1½-quart baking dish, with about a 1½-inch overhang. Transfer the crust to the prepared baking sheet. Cover the pastry with another piece of waxed paper and set aside in the freezer.

To prepare the filling, in a large skillet, combine the chicken, bay leaf, and peppercorns with water to cover. Bring to a simmer over medium-low heat and poach the chicken, partially covered, for 15 to 20 minutes. Allow the chicken to cool in the liquid. Remove the chicken and reserve 1 cup of the broth; discard the bay leaf and peppercorns. Cut the chicken into small chunks and set aside.

Melt the butter in a large saucepan over medium heat. Whisk in the flour. Cook, whisking occasionally, for 2 to 3 minutes. Gradually whisk in the reserved broth and continue to whisk until the sauce thickens. Remove the sauce from the heat and let cool slightly. Stir in the cream and Tabasco and season with salt and pepper.

Fold the smallest bits of chicken into the sauce. Place the remaining chunks of chicken in the bottom of the baking dish. Scatter the onions and peas over the chicken and pour in the sauce. Allow the mixture to cool completely. (The pot pie can be prepared up to this point, covered, and refrigerated for up to 2 days. Bring to room temperature before continuing.)

Preheat the oven to 450°F. Remove the pastry from the freezer and lightly brush the top with the beaten egg. Lay the crust flat on the top of the baking dish, egg-side down. The crust should not touch the filling. Brush the top with the egg and bake for 12 to 15 minutes. Reduce the oven temperature to 350°F and continue baking for about 35 minutes, until the crust is nicely browned and puffed up. Serve immediately.

❖ ROASTED TURKEY WITH CHIPOLATAS

SERVES 6 TO 8

1 turkey (about 14 pounds), liver reserved for the stuffing, and neck, gizzard, and heart reserved for the gravy

Salt and freshly ground black pepper, to taste

Cumberland Sausage Stuffing (recipe follows)

One 16-ounce can chestnuts, drained

1 cup (2 sticks) butter at room temperature

2 onions, chopped

2 carrots, chopped

1½ pounds chipolata or other small link sausages, roasted in the oven along with the turkey until browned

Giblet Gravy (recipe follows)

This traditional English Christmas dinner works just as well for Thanksgiving on this side of the Atlantic. Cumberland sausage is available at Myers of Keswick in New York City. If you can't make the trip to Myers, any other herbed sausage can be substituted.

Preheat the oven to 350°F. Season the turkey inside and out with salt and pepper. Fill the cavity with the stuffing, without packing it, and sew the opening closed with a large needle and kitchen string. Place the extra stuffing in a roasting dish, cover with foil, and refrigerate. Fill the neck cavity with the chestnuts and sew closed, being careful not to tear the skin.

Rub the turkey all over with some of the butter and place in a roasting pan. Surround with the onions and carrots. Roast for 2 hours, basting frequently with the remaining butter. Turn the oven temperature down to 250°F and roast for another 2 hours, until an instant-read thermometer inserted in the thigh reads 180°F. If the turkey becomes too brown, cover it loosely with heavy-duty foil.

Transfer the turkey to a large platter and let it rest for 20 to 30 minutes. Reserve the roasting pan to make the Giblet Gravy (page 96). Heat the extra stuffing in the oven while the turkey rests.

Remove and discard the trussing strings from the turkey and place the chipolatas around it. Serve with the extra stuffing and Giblet Gravy on the side.

Jane Ellis's Thanksgiving

CÉLERI RÉMOULADE (PAGE 14)

ROASTED TURKEY WITH CHIPOLATAS
CUMBERLAND SAUSAGE STUFFING • GIBLET GRAVY
CRANBERRY SALAD • ROASTED PARSNIPS • PUREED POTATOES
BRUSSELS SPROUTS • CREAMED ONIONS

PECAN PIE (PAGE 146) • JAMES BEARD'S PUMPKIN PIE (PAGE 146) •
AMBROSIA (PAGE 139)

CHAMPAGNE • BEAUJOLAIS NOUVEAU

CUMBERLAND SAUSAGE STUFFING

2 tablespoons butter

2 onions, chopped

2 garlic cloves, minced

1 1/2 pounds Cumberland sausage meat (or 3/4
    pound each ground pork and ground veal)

2 large eggs, beaten

Reserved turkey liver, sauteed in butter, flamed
    in Cognac, and finely chopped

1 cup plain bread crumbs

1/2 cup chopped pecans

2 tablespoons chopped fresh parsley

1 teaspoon ground cumin

1 teaspoon herbes de Provence

Several dashes Tabasco sauce

Salt and freshly ground black pepper, to taste

Melt the butter in a heavy skillet over medium-high heat. Sauté the onions and garlic for 4 to 5 minutes, until soft. Transfer to a large bowl and set aside.

In the same skillet, sauté the sausage meat, stirring, for about 5 minutes, until browned. Drain, discarding the fat. Transfer the sausage meat to the bowl with the onions and garlic. Add the eggs, liver, bread crumbs, pecans, parsley, cumin, herbes de Provence, Tabasco, salt, and pepper and blend well. Taste to correct the seasoning. (The stuffing can be prepared ahead and refrigerated for up to 1 day. Bring to room temperature before stuffing.)

GIBLET GRAVY

Reserved turkey neck, gizzard, and heart

1 large onion, halved

1 carrot, halved

1 celery stalk, halved

Fresh parsley sprigs

6 peppercorns

3 cups water

1 to 1 3/4 tablespoons all-purpose flour

2 tablespoons dry white wine or brandy
    (optional)

Salt and freshly ground black pepper, to taste

Combine the turkey neck, gizzard, and heart, the onion, carrot, celery, parsley, peppercorns, and water in a saucepan over medium-high heat. Bring to a boil and skim the surface of any scum. Reduce the heat to low and simmer for 30 minutes.

Strain the stock through a paper towel set in a strainer into a bowl. Reserve the neck, gizzard, and heart. You should have about 2 cups of stock. Dice the meat from the neck, gizzard, and heart and set aside.

When the turkey has finished roasting, place the roasting pan on top of the stove, over two burners if necessary. Skim off all but a few tablespoons of fat from the pan. Sprinkle the flour over the pan juices and whisk vigorously, scraping up the browned bits from the bottom of the pan. Gradually add the stock, whisking constantly over medium heat, until the gravy has thickened and is smooth. Strain into a saucepan and keep warm over low heat.

Add the wine, if using, the reserved giblets, and any juices from the serving platter to the gravy. Season with salt and pepper and serve with the turkey.

❖ ROASTED DUCK WITH WARM CHERRIES

SERVES 4

2 small ducks (about 3 pounds each)

1 tablespoon grated fresh ginger, plus 2 pieces ginger

Grated zest of ½ orange

Juice of 1 orange (reserve peel)

Juice of 2 lemons (reserve peels)

2 tablespoons apricot jam

1½ teaspoons crushed coriander seeds

1 teaspoon ground cinnamon

1 teaspoon freshly ground black pepper, or to taste

Salt, to taste

1 tablespoon vegetable oil

½ pound fresh cherries, split and pitted

1½ teaspoons butter

1 teaspoon sugar

Daniel Boulud of New York's Daniel restaurant serves this succulent duck along with Spinach Purée in Phyllo (page 124). If small ducks are not available, substitute two 4- to 5-pound ducks and increase the cooking time by ten minutes. If fresh cherries are not in season, substitute an 8-ounce can of dark cherries, rinsed, drained, and patted dry, and omit the sugar.

Preheat the oven to 450°F. Remove any loose fat from the ducks. To facilitate carving, cut out the wishbones. Place the ducks in a large pot and add enough water to cover by 2 inches. Bring to a boil and cook for 3 minutes. Drain thoroughly and let dry.

In a small bowl, combine the grated ginger, orange zest, orange juice, lemon juice, jam, coriander, cinnamon, and pepper. Set aside.

Prick the ducks all over with a sharp 2-tined fork, being careful to pierce just the skin, not the meat. Stuff each one with a piece of ginger and half the peels of the orange and lemons. Season the ducks inside and out with salt and pepper. Coat a roasting pan with the oil and add the ducks. Roast them in the center of the oven, basting every 5 minutes with the jam mixture, for 30 to 35 minutes, until the ducks are browned and crisp on the outside but still pink inside.

Remove the legs and breasts from the ducks and carve the breast meat into several thin slices. Put on a plate, cover loosely to keep warm, and set aside.

Meanwhile, combine the cherries, butter, and sugar in a small saucepan. Cook over medium heat for 5 to 8 minutes, until the cherries are slightly soft.

Arrange the slices of duck and legs on 4 plates, spoon the warm cherries on top, and serve.

Holiday Tabletops

At Hanukkah, the Jewish commemoration of the Maccabean recapturing and rededication of the Temple of Jerusalem, the dinner table (opposite) is decked out in the colors of the Israeli flag, sparkling with cobalt and platinum-stemmed glasses, silvery chargers, and snowy white orchids and linen.

For interior designer Victoria Hagan's Christmas office party (above), the table is set with Frette linens and antique crystal. The centerpiece compote is piled with pomander balls — oranges studded with cloves. Velvet ribbons, a little gold leaf tucked inside, dress up the napkins.

Kwanzaa, beginning the day after Christmas, is a seven-day celebration of African-American identity. The table (right) is set in colors as warm as the African earth, covered with a kuba cloth and decorated with corn and gourds.

❖ STILTON SIRLOIN BURGERS

SERVES 6

3 pounds ground sirloin

½ teaspoon kosher salt

6 Kaiser rolls, split, toasted, and buttered

3 to 4 ounces Stilton cheese, crumbled

Red pepper relish

1 small onion, thinly sliced

The hamburger gets a sophisticated twist at Bill Blass's country house, where it is served with a spoonful of crumbled Stilton cheese.

Preheat the oven to 180°F. Divide the sirloin into 6 equal parts and gently mold into patties. Sprinkle the salt into a large cast-iron frying pan and heat over medium-high heat. Add the burgers and cook, turning once, for 8 minutes for rare, 12 minutes for medium rare. Transfer the burgers to a baking dish and place in the preheated oven for 4 minutes.

Place the burgers on the rolls, top with the Stilton, relish, and onion, and serve.

The Glorious Fourth

TOMATO AND ONION SALAD

WATERCRESS SLAW

CHIPS • SALSA

STILTON SIRLOIN BURGERS

HOT DOGS

BAKED BEANS

EVELYN LAUDER'S POTATO SALAD (PAGE 114)

BEER • LEMONADE • WINE

STRAWBERRY SHORTCAKE WITH HOT CREAM SAUCE (PAGE 135)

WATERMELON

Evelyn and Leonard Lauder always fly the flag on Independence Day. The dining table, a riot of Americana, is backed by a quilt of Old Glory. On the table, antique flags form runners and little flags and pinwheels carry on the theme. Flowers, too, sing out the red, white, and blue.

❖ BILL BLASS'S MEAT LOAF

SERVES 6

2 pounds ground sirloin

½ pound ground veal

½ pound ground pork

2 tablespoons butter

2 celery stalks, chopped

1 large onion, chopped

1 large egg

1 tablespoon Worcestershire sauce

1½ cups soft fresh bread crumbs

½ cup chopped fresh parsley

⅓ cup sour cream

Pinch dried thyme

Pinch dried marjoram

Salt and freshly ground black pepper, to taste

1 bottle Heinz chili sauce

"I think my claim to immortality will be my meatloaf," says designer Bill Blass. "I'll never be remembered for my clothes." Not true, of course, but this recipe is certainly famous — and good. Perfect party food, it can be prepared ahead, and easily served. Blass likes it with mashed potatoes and succotash.

Preheat the oven to 350°F. In a large bowl, gently combine the sirloin, veal, and pork. Set aside.

Melt the butter in a skillet over medium-high heat. Sauté the celery and onion for about 10 minutes, until soft. Transfer to the bowl with the meat. Beat together the egg and Worcestershire and add to the meat, along with the bread crumbs, parsley, sour cream, thyme, marjoram, salt, and pepper. Combine well and form into a loaf.

Place the meat loaf in a baking dish and top with the chili sauce. Bake for 1 hour, or until cooked through. Serve.

❖ HERBED VEAL BUNDLES

SERVES 4

24 large butter or Boston lettuce leaves

¼ cup extra-virgin olive oil

4 scallions, finely chopped

¼ pound white mushrooms, finely chopped

2 garlic cloves, finely chopped

¼ cup finely chopped fresh parsley

1 pound ground veal

Salt and freshly ground black pepper, to taste

6 tablespoons freshly grated Parmesan cheese

2 large eggs, lightly beaten

2 cups white wine or chicken broth

¼ cup finely chopped fresh herbs, such as
    thyme, oregano, and/or tarragon

Gently blanched lettuce leaves make a nice wrap for seasoned minced veal. The key to the flavor of this dish, says Emalee Chapman, is the garnish of fresh herbs: Use your favorite, or choose whatever looks the freshest at the market or the brightest in your garden.

In a large pot of boiling water, blanch the lettuce leaves, 2 or 3 at a time, for about 1 second, just to soften. Drain on paper towels and set aside.

Heat the olive oil in a large skillet over medium heat. Sauté the scallions for 2 minutes, or until softened. Add the mushrooms, garlic, and parsley and sauté for 1 minute, stirring. Add the veal and sauté for 2 minutes. Season with salt and pepper and stir in the Parmesan. Remove from the heat and let cool for about 2 minutes. Add the eggs and blend well.

Lay a lettuce leaf on a work surface and spoon 1 tablespoon of the filling along 1 edge. Roll the lettuce around the filling and set aside, seam-side down, on a plate. Repeat with the remaining lettuce and filling.

Place the lettuce bundles seam-side down, in a large skillet. Add the wine and bring to a simmer over low heat. Cover and simmer for 15 minutes.

Place the bundles on a serving platter, spoon the sauce from the pan over them, and garnish with the herbs. Serve.

❖ LAMB STEW WITH NEW POTATOES

SERVES 4

4 tablespoons olive oil

3 tablespoons butter

2 carrots, diced

2 large onions, diced

I bone-in lamb shoulder, about 3¹/₂ pounds
    (have the butcher cut it into 12 pieces)

2 tablespoons all-purpose flour

I tablespoon tomato paste

2 cups water

2 cups veal stock

3 garlic cloves, finely chopped

I bouquet garni of I bay leaf, I fresh parsley
    sprig, and I fresh thyme sprig, tied together
    with kitchen string

I cup canned tomatoes, coarsely chopped, with
    their juice

Salt and freshly ground black pepper, to taste

³/₄ pound small new potatoes, peeled

Braising — cooking at a low temperature for a long time — is the heart and soul of bistro fare. It turns inexpensive cuts of meat and simple vegetables into great dishes — like this lamb stew with new potatoes from the Ritz-Escoffier cooking school in Paris. And the beautiful thing about stew is that it's almost always better the second day.

In a 6-quart Dutch oven or a large heavy pot, heat 2 tablespoons of the olive oil and 1 tablespoon of the butter over medium heat. Sauté the carrots and onions for about 8 minutes, until lightly browned. Set aside.

Preheat the oven to 425°F. Heat the remaining 2 tablespoons olive oil and 2 tablespoons butter in a large skillet. Add the lamb and cook, turning occasionally, for 8 to 10 minutes, until well browned on all sides. Transfer the lamb to the Dutch oven, sprinkle with the flour, and mix in the tomato paste. Bake for 10 minutes.

Add the water and stock to the Dutch oven and place over high heat. Bring to a boil and skim the surface. Stir in the garlic, bouquet garni, and tomatoes and their juice. Season with salt and pepper. Cover and bake for 50 minutes, or until the lamb begins to come away from the bones. With tongs, transfer the lamb to a large bowl and set aside. Strain the sauce through a paper towel set in a strainer into another large pot.

In a saucepan, combine the potatoes with enough water to cover and add 1 teaspoon salt. Bring to a boil over medium-high heat and boil for 1 minute. Drain and add the potatoes to the sauce. Bring to a simmer over medium heat and cook for 15 to 20 minutes, until the potatoes are tender.

Remove any loosened bones from the lamb and add the meat to the sauce. Simmer until heated through and serve.

❖ SHEPHERD'S PIE

SERVES 6

3 tablespoons vegetable oil

2 onions, finely chopped

3 carrots, finely chopped

2 garlic cloves, minced

1¾ pounds ground lamb

3 tablespoons tomato paste

1 cup lamb or beef broth

2 tablespoons Worcestershire sauce

Salt and freshly ground black pepper, to taste

1 teaspoon herbes de Provence (or a mixture
        of dried herbs such as thyme, rosemary,
        tarragon, bay leaf, and/or savory)

3 large all-purpose potatoes, peeled

1 cup milk

½ cup (1 stick) butter

2 tablespoons freshly grated Parmesan cheese

England's favorite nursery food, shepherd's pie is a great prepare-ahead party dish for grown-ups. It's also a wonderful warming one-dish meal for casual winter gatherings. The meat filling can be made two days ahead and gently reheated in the oven before completing the dish by adding the mashed potatoes and baking.

Heat the oil in a large skillet over low heat. Sauté the onions, carrots, and garlic for about 10 minutes, until soft. Raise the heat to medium, add the lamb, and cook, stirring, until it is well browned.

Drain off the fat from the pan and discard. Add the tomato paste, broth, and Worcestershire and mix well. Season with salt and pepper. Stir in the herbs and cook, stirring occasionally, for 15 minutes. Set aside.

Meanwhile, in a large pot, combine the potatoes with cold water to cover. Bring to a boil and cook for about 30 minutes, until tender. Drain well and mash.

Meanwhile, heat the milk in a small pot over medium heat until small bubbles begin to appear around the edges. Add the butter in small pieces, stirring until absorbed. Season with salt and pepper.

Stir the milk mixture into the mashed potatoes.

Preheat the oven to 350°F. Lightly butter a large baking dish. Spread the meat mixture evenly across the bottom of the dish. Spread the mashed potatoes on top so that the meat is completely covered. Run a fork over the top so the tines create ridges. Sprinkle with the Parmesan. Bake, uncovered, for 35 minutes. If the top is not golden brown, place the pie under the broiler for about 1 minute to brown. Serve.

❖ BRAISED LAMB SHANKS

SERVES 4

2 to 3 tablespoons olive oil

4 bone-in lamb shanks (about 1 pound each)

³/₄ cup red wine, or more if necessary

¹/₄ cup pitted oil-cured black olives

2 garlic cloves, halved

2 to 3 fresh rosemary sprigs, plus more
for garnish

Salt and freshly ground black pepper, to taste

*This hearty winter dish, highly popular on restaurant menus these days, is
served with a white bean purée by designer Linda Allard. The shanks can be
cooked an hour or two ahead and reheated gently before serving.*

In a heavy pot large enough to hold the lamb shanks comfortably,
heat the oil. Add the lamb and cook, turning occasionally, for 8 to
10 minutes, until well browned on all sides.

Add the wine, olives, garlic, and rosemary. Season with salt and
pepper. Reduce the heat to low, cover, and simmer for 1¹/₂ to 2
hours, until the shanks are tender; as they cook, check that there is
about ¹/₂ inch of liquid in the casserole and add more wine or water
as necessary.

Remove and discard the rosemary. Transfer the shanks to a serving platter and pour the pan juices over the top. Garnish with fresh
rosemary sprigs and serve.

*Linda Allard's
Hearty Sunday Supper*

ROASTED RED PEPPER SOUP (PAGE 42)

BRAISED LAMB SHANKS
WHITE BEAN PURÉE
MIXED WINTER GREENS WITH BACON (PAGE 121)

HOME BAKED BREAD

MIXED SALAD WITH VINAIGRETTE

MERLOT

RUSTIC APPLE TART (PAGE 144)
CAPPUCCINO

❖ GARLIC-CILANTRO PORK TENDERLOIN

SERVES 4

½ cup chopped fresh cilantro, plus more
    for garnish

¼ cup olive oil

3 tablespoons fresh lime juice

4 garlic cloves, minced

Freshly ground black pepper, to taste

1½ pounds pork tenderloin, cut crosswise into
    1-inch pieces and pounded to flatten slightly

1 tablespoon vegetable oil

Pork tenderloin is a great choice for a party menu: A good marinade gives it terrific flavor, and it's a snap to cook and serve. If you don't care for the taste of cilantro, try this with fresh thyme instead.

In a shallow dish, combine the cilantro, olive oil, lime juice, garlic, and pepper. Add the pork, turning to coat. Cover with plastic wrap and refrigerate for at least 4 hours, or overnight. Remove the pork from the marinade, discarding the marinade.

Heat the vegetable oil in a large skillet over medium-high heat. Add the pork and cook, turning once, for 4 to 5 minutes, until cooked through but still pink. Garnish with cilantro and serve.

❖ PORK ROASTED IN BEER

SERVES 8 TO 10

One 6-pound boneless center-cut pork loin
    roast, well trimmed, rolled, and tied

2 tablespoons safflower oil

2 tablespoons coarse sea salt

1 tablespoon peppercorns

1 tablespoon caraway seeds

Three 12-ounce bottles light beer

1 vegetable bouillon cube, crushed

2 large fresh sage sprigs

Austrian-born Renate McKnight remembers this roast pork with beer-flavored gravy from her childhood. It's a great party dish, as it can be made up to two days ahead and reheated at serving time.

Preheat the oven to 450°F. Lightly coat the pork with oil on all sides and place, fatty-side up, in a shallow roasting pan.

Process the salt, peppercorns, and caraway seeds until coarsely chopped in a food processor. Sprinkle two thirds of the mixture over the top and sides of the pork. Roast on the middle oven rack for 15 minutes. Add 2 bottles of the beer and the bouillon and sage. Reduce the oven temperature to 350°F and roast, basting frequently and adding more beer if necessary, for about 1 hour, until an instant-read meat thermometer inserted in the center of the roast reads 155°F. Transfer the pork to a platter and let rest for 15 minutes. (The pork can be prepared to this point and refrigerated for up to 2 days. Reheat in a 300°F oven for 45 minutes, basting occasionally.)

Add the remaining beer (or about 1 cup water) to the pan along with the remaining spice mixture. Place the pan over medium-low heat and simmer for about 10 minutes, until the liquid is reduced. Slice the roast and serve with the hot gravy on the side.

❖GRILLED PORK CHOPS AND APPLES

SERVES 6

1¹/₄ cups apple cider

1¹/₂ tablespoons olive oil

1 tablespoon cider vinegar

1 tablespoon coarse Dijon mustard

¹/₂ teaspoon ground cumin

¹/₄ teaspoon ground coriander

3 crushed black mushrooms

2 small garlic cloves, crushed

1 teaspoon crushed red pepper flakes
(optional)

Salt and freshly ground black pepper, to taste

6 boneless loin pork chops, about ¹/₂-inch thick

1 teaspoon unsalted butter

1 large yellow onion, sliced into 1/4-inch rings

¹/₂ teaspoon sugar

1 teaspoon balsamic vinegar

2 apples, peeled, cored, and cut into
¹/₄-inch slices

These pork chops come from Dodie Ellis of Santa Fe who likes to serve them accompanied by a tomato salad with a cumin seed vinaigrette. The chops get their great flavor from the spicy marinade in which they sit overnight.

In a bowl, combine 1 cup of the cider, the olive oil, vinegar, mustard, cumin, coriander, mushrooms, garlic, red pepper flakes, if using, salt and pepper. Place the pork chops in a large shallow glass dish and pour the marinade over them to coat evenly. Cover the dish with plastic wrap and refrigerate overnight, turning the chops several times.

Melt the butter in a large nonstick skillet over low heat. Add the onion, raise the heat to medium-high, and sauté, stirring occasionally, for about 10 minutes, until it begins to brown. Add the remaining ¹/₄ cup apple cider and the sugar and stir to combine. Reduce the heat to low and cook, stirring frequently, for 15 to 20 minutes, until the onion has caramelized. Stir in the balsamic vinegar and remove the pan from the heat.

Meanwhile, remove the pork chops from the refrigerator and bring to room temperature. Preheat the grill to high and brush with oil. Remove the pork chops from the marinade and grill them, loosely covered with foil, for 10 to 12 minutes, turning once. Transfer to a large heated platter and keep warm.

Place the apple slices in a grill basket and grill, turning once, for about 2 minutes, until browned and softened.

Garnish the pork chops with the caramelized onions and grilled apples and serve.

❖ CASSOULET

SERVES 6 TO 8

1 duck (4 to 5 pounds), excess fat removed
    from cavity

1 pound fatback or bacon, cut into ¼-inch slices

1 pound merguez sausage or other hot sausage

1 pound garlic sausage

2 pounds boneless lamb shoulder, cut into
    2-inch cubes

3 onions, diced

1 garlic head, cloves separated, peeled, and
    cut in half

8 cups water

2 pounds Great Northern or other white beans,
    soaked in water overnight and drained

5 fresh thyme sprigs

1 bay leaf

Salt and freshly ground black pepper, to taste

½ loaf day-old French bread, crusts discarded
    and bread torn into pieces

¼ cup chopped fresh parsley

1 tablespoon chopped fresh thyme

*The ideal dish for a cold winter night, cassoulet can be made ahead —
and it's better if it is. Henry Meer's version is simple, as it doesn't call for
a duck confit, just duck and shoulder of lamb. Link or Italian
sausage can replace the hot sausage, and bacon can replace the fatback.
All it needs as an accompaniment is a tossed salad.*

Preheat the oven to 400°F. Put the duck on a rack in a roasting pan and roast for 50 minutes. Cool. Remove the duck breasts and legs and cut the meat into 2- to 3-inch pieces. Reserve.

In a large skillet over medium heat, cook the fatback until it has rendered its fat and is golden brown. Remove with a slotted spoon and reserve. Pour the fat into a container and reserve.

Heat 1 tablespoon of the reserved fat in a skillet over medium heat. Add the sausage and cook, turning, until browned on all sides, about 10 minutes. Slice into ½-inch pieces and set aside. In a clean skillet, heat another tablespoon of the reserved fat and cook the garlic sausage; slice and set aside. Repeat to brown the lamb on all sides; set aside.

Reduce the oven temperature to 350°F. Heat 2 tablespoons of the reserved fat in a 4-quart flameproof casserole over medium heat. Sauté the onions and garlic for 5 to 6 minutes, until the onions are translucent. Add the lamb, water, beans, thyme sprig, bay leaf, salt, and pepper and bring to a boil. Boil for 10 minutes and skim the surface.

Cover and bake until the beans are tender but not mushy, about 1½ hours; stir the cassoulet a couple of times to prevent sticking. If the beans have absorbed most of the liquid, add 1 cup hot water to the casserole and stir thoroughly.

Meanwhile, in a food processor, combine the bread, parsley, and chopped thyme and process to crumbs.

Fold the duck pieces into the casserole. Place the sausage and fatback on top and cover with an even layer of the bread crumbs. Bake the cassoulet, uncovered, for about 45 minutes, or until a crust forms on top. Serve.

❖SEARED THREE-PEPPER VENISON CHOPS WITH THREE-LILY JAM

SERVES 8

3 cups dry red wine

6 tablespoons olive oil

¼ cup crushed cranberries

2 garlic cloves, smashed

8 loin venison chops (about ½ pound each)

1 tablespoon crushed white peppercorns

1 tablespoon crushed red peppercorns

1 tablespoon crushed green peppercorns

Three-Lily Jam (recipe follows)

¼ cup Cranberry Oil (recipe follows)

Fresh flat-leaf parsley leaves, for garnish

In this elegant presentation, Marjorie and Ellery Gordon's peppered venison is combined with cranberry oil and an onion compote (onions, shallots, and leeks are the three lilies in question). Swiss Chard Timbales (page 126) would round out the feast. Venison, a low-fat alternative to beef, has a slight gamey flavor. It is available in larger meat markets.

In a large bowl, combine the wine, 2 tablespoons of the olive oil, the cranberries, and garlic. Add the venison chops, turning to coat. Cover with plastic wrap and refrigerate for 24 hours. Remove from the refrigerator 2 hours before cooking.

Preheat the oven to 450°F. Combine the white, red, and green peppercorns on a plate. Remove the chops from the marinade and press both sides of each chop into the peppercorns. Reserve the marinade.

Heat the remaining 4 tablespoons olive oil in a large sauté pan over medium-high heat. Sear the chops, turning once, for 3 minutes, until golden brown on both sides. Transfer the chops to a roasting pan, and roast 10 minutes for medium-rare, or to desired doneness.

Meanwhile, add the reserved marinade to the sauté pan and boil, scraping up any browned bits, until reduced to about ½ cup.

Place 2 tablespoons of the Three-Lily Jam on each of 8 warmed dinner plates, top with the venison chops, and drizzle the reduced marinade on top. Drizzle 1½ teaspoons Cranberry Oil beside each chop, garnish with parsley, and serve.

THREE-LILY JAM

MAKES ABOUT 2 CUPS

$1/4$ cup canola oil
2 large Spanish onions, thinly sliced
10 shallots, thinly sliced
4 leeks, white part only, thinly sliced and
    well washed
1 cup red wine
$1/2$ cup granulated sugar
$1/2$ cup packed light brown sugar
$1/2$ cup balsamic vinegar

Heat the oil in a large skillet over medium-high heat. Sauté the onions, shallots, and leeks for 6 to 8 minutes, stirring occasionally, until translucent. Add the wine, granulated sugar, brown sugar, and vinegar and cook, stirring, until the sugars dissolve. Reduce the heat to low and cook, stirring occasionally, until all the liquid has evaporated. (The jam can be prepared ahead, tightly covered, and refrigerated for several days. Warm in a saucepan over low heat before serving.)

CRANBERRY OIL

MAKES ABOUT $3/4$ CUP

2 cups cranberry juice
$1/2$ cup canola oil
2 shallots, thinly sliced

In a saucepan over medium-high heat, simmer the cranberry juice until reduced to $1/4$ cup. Set aside.

Heat the oil in a skillet over medium-low heat. Sauté the shallots for 3 to 4 minutes, until translucent. Let cool for 10 minutes.

Strain the oil through a fine strainer into a blender, add the reduced cranberry juice, and blend for 30 seconds. (The cranberry oil can be prepared ahead, tightly covered, and refrigerated for several days. Bring to room temperature before serving.)

Side Dishes

❖ MASHED POTATOES WITH HERBS

SERVES 6 TO 8

6 large russet potatoes, peeled and quartered
¹/₂ cup (1 stick) butter
²/₃ cup extra-virgin olive oil
¹/₂ cup fresh lemon juice
¹/₂ cup dry white wine
1 tablespoon finely chopped fresh rosemary
1 tablespoon finely chopped fresh thyme
Salt and freshly ground black pepper, to taste

Rosemary and thyme, plus a squeeze of fresh lemon, give these mashed potatoes a tangy freshness. In this recipe from Meaghan Dowling, the potatoes are broken up with an old-fashioned potato masher, then finished with a wooden spoon.

In a large pot, combine the potatoes with cold salted water to cover. Bring to a boil and cook until just tender, 20 to 30 minutes. Drain.

Return the potatoes to the pot and mash them with a potato masher. Place over low heat and add the butter, olive oil, lemon juice, wine, rosemary, thyme, salt, and pepper. Cook, stirring with a wooden spoon, until the butter is melted and all the ingredients are thoroughly incorporated. Serve.

❖ GREEN CHILE COUNTRY-STYLE POTATOES

SERVES 4 TO 6

3 carrots, quartered
5 russet potatoes, peeled and quartered
¹/₃ cup sour cream
¹/₄ cup (¹/₂ stick) unsalted butter at room temperature
¹/₂ cup chopped green chile peppers (wear gloves when handling chile peppers)
4 scallions, white and 2 inches of green parts, chopped
5 dashes Tabasco sauce, or more to taste
Pinch ground red pepper, or more to taste
Kosher salt and freshly ground black pepper, to taste

Green chiles, scallions, and a generous dash of Tabasco sauce make sure this dish delivers a true southwestern zing. It's from Michael Fennelly of Santacafé in Santa Fe.

In a large pot, combine the carrots and potatoes with cold salted water to cover. Bring to a boil and cook until the vegetables are tender, about 25 minutes. Drain, transfer to a serving bowl, and coarsely mash with a potato masher. Add the sour cream, butter, chiles, scallions, Tabasco, red pepper, 1 teaspoon of salt, and ¹/₂ teaspoon of black pepper and continue to mash until the desired smoothness is reached. Taste to correct seasoning and serve.

❖ EVELYN LAUDER'S POTATO SALAD

SERVES 4 TO 6

1 pound small red potatoes

1/4 teaspoon caraway seeds

1/4 cup Dijon mustard

2 tablespoons water

1 tablespoon fresh lemon juice

2 teaspoons honey

2 tablespoons vegetable oil

2 tablespoons green pickle relish

1 small onion, diced

4 slices crisp bacon, crumbled (optional)

Leonard and Evelyn Lauder love to celebrate the Fourth of July, and Evelyn's mustardy potato salad is always a part of the festivities. The salad is best if served warm, but it can also be brought to the picnic table at room temperature.

In a large pot, combine the potatoes and caraway seeds with cold salted water to cover. Bring to a boil and cook for about 15 minutes, until just tender. Drain and let cool slightly.

In a small bowl, whisk together the mustard, water, lemon juice, honey, and oil. Stir in the relish and set aside.

When the potatoes are cool enough to handle, cut each in half (quarters if they are a little large) and place in a serving bowl. Add the onion and mix carefully. Add the bacon, if using. Pour the mustard mixture over the potatoes, toss gently to coat, and serve warm.

❖ SWEET POTATO PURÉE

SERVES 4 TO 6

1 tablespoon olive oil

2 shallots, diced

3/4 cup orange juice

2 1/4 pounds sweet potatoes

2 tablespoons butter

Salt and freshly ground black pepper, to taste

Puréed sweet potatoes, flavored with orange, make an unusually good accompaniment to fish, turkey, or chicken. This recipe comes from David Page of Home restaurant in New York City.

Heat the olive oil in a large saucepan over medium heat. Sauté the shallots for about 5 minutes, until translucent. Add the orange juice, bring to a simmer, and simmer until reduced by half. Set aside.

In a large pot, combine the sweet potatoes with cold salted water to cover. Bring to a boil and cook until tender, about 30 minutes. Drain. Peel when just cool enough to handle.

In the bowl of a standing mixer fitted with the paddle attachment, combine the sweet potatoes, orange juice mixture, and butter. Season with salt and pepper. Beat until puréed (or mash together all the ingredients with a potato masher), adding warm water if necessary to reach the desired consistency. Transfer to a large bowl and serve.

❖ SAFFRON RICE

SERVES 4 TO 6

1 tablespoon butter
1 onion, chopped
2 cups water
½ teaspoon salt
¼ teaspoon freshly ground black pepper
Pinch saffron threads
1 cup long-grain rice

In this simple recipe from the Outermost Inn, a little saffron gives this rice a wonderful golden tone and a great taste boost. Serve it alongside grilled fish or chicken.

Preheat the oven to 350°F. Melt the butter in a heavy flameproof casserole over medium heat. Sauté the onion for about 4 to 5 minutes, until soft. Add the water, salt, pepper, and saffron. Bring to a boil, remove from the heat, and let sit for 5 minutes.

Return saffron water to a boil and add the rice. Cover and bake for 15 minutes, until the rice has absorbed all of the liquid and is tender. Transfer to a serving bowl and serve.

❖ GRITS SOUFFLÉ

SERVES 8 TO 10

2¼ cups milk
2¼ cups water
1 cup old-fashioned grits
1 pound cheddar cheese, coarsely grated
Salt and freshly ground black pepper, to taste
5 large eggs, separated, at room temperature

John Rosselli's friends are mad about this Southern dish. So is John: It is easy to make and the perfect side dish for chicken or lamb.

Preheat the oven to 350°F. Bring the milk and water to a boil in a nonstick saucepan over medium heat. Slowly stir in the grits. Reduce the heat to low, cover, and cook, stirring occasionally, for 12 to 14 minutes, until thickened. Remove the pan from the heat, add the cheese, and mix until thoroughly incorporated. Season with salt and pepper.

Stir the egg yolks into the grits mixture. In a bowl with an electric mixer, beat the egg whites until soft peaks form (do not overbeat). Gently fold the egg whites into the grits mixture. Spoon the mixture into a 9x14x2-inch baking dish. Bake for 1 to 1½ hours, until the top is lightly browned and crisp at the edges. Serve.

❖ WILD RICE WITH PORCINI DUXELLES

SERVES 6

1 ½ cups wild rice, rinsed and picked over

½ ounce dried porcini mushrooms

1 cup warm water

2 shallots, coarsely chopped

2 tablespoons olive oil

⅓ cup white wine

½ to 1 cup chicken broth

Salt and freshly ground black pepper, to taste

2 tablespoons unsalted butter

¼ cup chopped fresh parsley

Endive leaves, for garnish

This earthy combination of wild rice and porcini mushrooms, served by Michael Trapp, is exceptionally good with game birds. It can be made ahead and reheated gently in a double boiler before the butter and parsley are added.

In a small bowl, combine the rice with 1 ½ cups boiling water. Cover and soak for 1 hour. Drain. Rinse and drain again. Set aside.

Meanwhile, in a small bowl, soak the mushrooms in the warm water for 1 hour. Remove the mushrooms from the soaking liquid and squeeze out the excess moisture. Reserve the mushroom liquid. In a food processor, combine the mushrooms and shallots and process until minced. Heat the olive oil in a large skillet over medium heat. Sauté the mushroom mixture, stirring constantly, for 2 minutes. Add the rice and cook, stirring, for 2 minutes. Add the wine and cook until the wine has almost completely evaporated. Add the reserved mushroom liquid and ½ cup of the broth, cover, and simmer for about 25 minutes, until the rice has absorbed the liquid. Test after 20 minutes for doneness. The rice should be tender but not mushy. If the rice is still crunchy, add the remaining ½ cup chicken broth and continue to simmer until it is tender.

Season the rice with salt and pepper, stir in the butter and parsley, and mix well. Transfer to a serving platter, garnish with endive leaves, and serve.

❖ROASTED VEGETABLES

SERVES 8

3 tablespoons olive oil

3 garlic cloves

8 carrots, cut into 1-inch pieces

16 small Brussels sprouts

8 new potatoes, halved

2 large onions, coarsely chopped

1 green bell pepper, cored, seeded, and cut
    into ½-inch cubes

2 leeks, cut into ½-inch pieces and well washed

2 eggplants, halved, seeded, and cut into ½-inch
    cubes

Fresh basil leaves, for garnish

*Roasting vegetables concentrates their flavors by the simplest means using the
minimum of fat. It is an excellent way to cook them, especially for a crowd,
and they're just about perfect with any roast meat or fowl.*

Preheat the oven to 350°F. Combine the olive oil and garlic in a
large roasting pan and roast for 5 minutes. Add the carrots,
Brussels sprouts, and potatoes and roast, turning occasionally, for
15 to 20 minutes, until the vegetables are barely tender. Add the
onions, pepper, leeks, and eggplant and roast, turning occasionally,
for 20 to 30 minutes, until the vegetables are lightly browned and
crisp on the edges. Transfer the vegetables to a serving platter, garnish with the basil, and serve.

❖ ROASTED LEEKS

SERVES 6

2 tablespoons olive oil

12 leeks, split lengthwise, and well washed

Salt and freshly ground black pepper, to taste

Chopped fresh parsley, chervil, or tarragon,
    for garnish

*Garnished with roasted garlic and herbs, roasted leeks make a great
addition to the Thanksgiving meal, or a garnish for roasted meats or fish.
The recipe is courtesy of Tom Colicchio of the Gramercy Tavern.*

Preheat the oven to 375°F. Drizzle 1 tablespoon of the olive oil over the bottom of a large roasting pan. Add the leeks, cut-side down. Season with salt and pepper. Drizzle the remaining 1 tablespoon olive oil over the leeks. Roast until browned and tender, about 40 minutes. Garnish with the herbs and serve.

❖ CAULIFLOWER WITH FRESH HERB VINAIGRETTE

SERVES 4

2 small cauliflower heads, separated into florets

⅓ cup extra-virgin olive oil

2 tablespoons white wine vinegar

1 tablespoon fresh lemon juice

1 tablespoon capers, finely chopped

1 tablespoon chopped fresh parsley, plus more
    for garnish

1 teaspoon chopped fresh tarragon

1 teaspoon chopped fresh oregano

1 teaspoon chopped fresh thyme

1 garlic clove, finely chopped

Salt and freshly ground black pepper, to taste

*Cauliflower, the king of cabbages, takes on a new dimension when
it is drizzled with a fresh herb vinaigrette. Though delicious hot from the
steamer, the dish can also be made ahead and served at room
temperature, after allowing the cauliflower to pick up more flavor from
the vinaigrette.*

In a vegetable steamer over boiling water, steam the cauliflower for 12 to 15 minutes, until tender. Transfer to a serving plate.

In a small bowl, combine the olive oil, vinegar, lemon juice, capers, parsley, tarragon, oregano, thyme, and garlic. Season with salt and pepper.

Quickly whisk the vinaigrette, pour it over the cauliflower, and toss. Garnish with parsley and serve.

❖ MOROCCAN SPICED CARROTS WITH CUMIN-HONEY VINAIGRETTE

SERVES 4

Vegetables:

3 tablespoons olive oil

1 large onion, sliced into ¼-inch rings

10 carrots, cut diagonally into ⅛-inch slices

24 Moroccan black olives

8 slices Preserved Lemons (recipe follows)

Paprika, to taste

Ground red pepper, to taste

Salt and freshly ground black pepper, to taste

Dressing:

2 tablespoons fresh lemon juice

2 teaspoons honey

2 teaspoons ground cumin

1 teaspoon chopped fresh mint

¼ cup olive oil

Salt and freshly ground black pepper, to taste

1 teaspoon toasted cumin seeds, for garnish

Honey and cumin in the vinaigrette spice up this salad of carrots, preserved lemons, and black olives from Matthew Kenney. It can be served as part of a Moroccan meze table — an array of spicy appetizers and salads (page 52) — or as a side dish, or on its own as a first course.

To prepare the vegetables, heat 1 tablespoon of the olive oil in a large nonstick skillet over high heat. Sauté the onion, turning once, for about 6 minutes, until translucent. Remove from the skillet, coarsely chop, and set aside.

Heat the remaining 2 tablespoons olive oil in the skillet over high heat. Add the carrots and cook for about 5 minutes, until well browned. Reduce the heat to medium and cook until the carrots are tender, about 2 minutes. Stir in the onions, olives, and preserved lemon. Season with paprika, red pepper, salt, and black pepper. Remove from the heat and set aside.

To prepare the dressing, in a small bowl, whisk together the lemon juice, honey, cumin, and mint. Slowly whisk in the olive oil. Season with salt and pepper. Pour the dressing over the carrots and toss well. Garnish with the cumin seeds and serve.

PRESERVED LEMONS

5 lemons

¼ cup salt

Cinnamon stick, cloves, star anise, coriander seeds, bay leaves, and/or
    black peppercorns (optional)

Make 8 incisions in the peel of each lemon, but do not cut as deep as the membrane. Place the lemons in a stainless-steel saucepan with the salt and enough water to cover. Gently boil until the lemon peels become soft, about 12 minutes. Pack the lemons and spices, if using, into a clean 1-pint jar. Fill with enough saltwater from the pan to cover. Close the jar tightly with a lid and let sit for 5 days. Store in the refrigerator for up to 1 month.

❖SAUTÉED SALSIFY WITH BACON, MUSHROOMS, AND PEARL ONIONS

SERVES 6

4 cups chicken broth

6 salsify, peeled

4 garlic cloves

2 fresh thyme sprigs, plus chopped thyme for garnish

18 pearl onions, peeled

4 ounces slab bacon, sliced into 2-inch long matchsticks

¼ pound chanterelle mushrooms

¼ pound black trumpet mushrooms

Salt and freshly ground black pepper, to taste

Salsify — a root vegetable with a delicate flavor some say is reminiscent of asparagus, artichoke, and oysters (it's also called oyster plant) — is tossed with bacon, mushrooms, and onions, in this side dish from Tom Colicchio. Watch the salsify carefully: Overcooking turns it mushy.

Bring the broth to a simmer in a saucepan over medium heat. Add the salsify, garlic, and thyme sprigs and cook for 5 to 7 minutes, until the salsify is just tender. (Be careful not to overcook.) Remove the salsify with a slotted spoon and cut into 2-inch pieces.

Add the onions to the broth and cook until soft, 10 to 15 minutes. Drain and discard the broth (or reserve for another use).

In a large skillet over medium heat, cook the bacon until browned. Stir in the salsify, onions, and mushrooms. Sauté for 6 to 8 minutes, until the mushrooms are browned. Season with salt and pepper, garnish with chopped thyme, and serve.

❖ MIXED WINTER GREENS WITH BACON

SERVES 4

1 pound assorted winter greens such as kale,
    turnip greens, mustard greens, spinach,
    Swiss chard, and/or dandelion

2 strips bacon

1 tablespoon honey

Winter greens like kale, turnip greens, mustard greens, spinach, and Swiss chard become a delicious dish when they're tossed in a skillet with a little bacon fat. The recipe comes from Barbara Damrosch who grows vegetables in Maine throughout the year.

Wash and shake the greens dry, leaving some moisture on leaves. If using kale or chard, remove the thick center ribs.

In a large skillet over medium heat, cook the bacon until lightly browned. Remove from the pan, break into small pieces, and set aside.

Drain the excess fat from the skillet. Add the greens and cook over medium heat, covered, for about 2 minutes, until just tender. Stir in the honey and bacon and serve.

❖ ROASTED RED AND YELLOW PEPPERS

SERVES 6

4 red bell peppers

4 yellow bell peppers

3 tablespoons olive oil

Pinch salt

This colorful melange of peppers, an interesting side dish Michael Trapp serves with game hens at holiday parties, would go well with roasted meats and fish.

Roast the peppers over a gas or charcoal flame, or under a broiler, turning occasionally, for 15 minutes, or until blackened on all sides. Transfer to a plastic bag, seal tightly, and steam for 10 minutes. When cool enough to handle, peel, core, and seed the peppers. Slice the peppers into large strips. (The peppers can be prepared to this point, covered, and refrigerated overnight.)

Heat the olive oil in a large skillet over medium heat. Add the peppers and heat for 3 to 4 minutes, until hot. Season with salt and serve.

❖ SUCCOTASH

SERVES 6

1 teaspoon butter

2 cups cooked corn

1 cup cooked lima beans

1 teaspoon sugar

1 cup heavy cream

1/2 teaspoon salt

1/4 teaspoon freshly ground black pepper

This homey lima bean and corn dish is served by Bill Blass with his legendary meatloaf (page 102). The limas can be fresh or frozen.

Melt the butter in a medium saucepan over medium-low heat. Add the corn, lima beans, and sugar, mixing to coat the vegetables well. Stir in the cream, a little bit at a time, and continue to stir until the mixture thickens, about 5 minutes. Season with the salt and pepper and serve.

❖ ROASTED PEPPERS STUFFED WITH WALNUTS

SERVES 8

2 tablespoons olive oil

6 red bell peppers, cut lengthwise in thirds, cored, and seeded

One 14 1/2-ounce can chunky tomatoes, drained

4 anchovy fillets, soaked in water for 15 minutes, drained, and finely chopped

1/4 cup chopped fresh basil (or 1 teaspoon dried)

4 shallots, minced

2 tablespoons capers, rinsed

2 tablespoons freshly grated Parmesan cheese

1/4 cup chopped walnuts

Freshly ground black pepper, to taste

Peppers stuffed with anchovies, basil, and walnuts make a good summer vegetable dish to serve warm or cold. Joe Famularo, cookbook author and entertaining expert, likes to garnish the platter with a variety of hot peppers.

Preheat the oven to 400°F. Rub or brush the oil over the inside and outside of the bell peppers. Arrange the peppers on a baking sheet, skin-side down.

In a bowl, combine the tomatoes, anchovies, basil, shallots, and capers. Place a generous teaspoon of the mixture in each pepper piece. Bake for 20 minutes.

Sprinkle with the Parmesan, walnuts, and black pepper and bake for 10 minutes more. Place under the a preheated broiler for 2 to 3 minutes, until the edges of the peppers are slightly charred. Serve hot or just warm.

❖ SHALLOTS IN RED WINE

SERVES 8

3 tablespoons olive oil

12 shallots, peeled

¾ cup vegetable or chicken broth

1 teaspoon sugar

1 fresh rosemary sprig

Salt and freshly ground white pepper, to taste

1 cup red wine

3 tablespoons butter

Shallots cooked in red wine until they are sweet and tender go well with a robust entrée such as Lamb Stew with New Potatoes (page 104). The recipe comes from the West Street Grill.

Heat the olive oil in a skillet over medium heat. Add the shallots and cook, turning occasionally, until golden on all sides, about 15 minutes. Add the broth, sugar, and rosemary and season with salt and white pepper. Raise the heat to high and cook until the cooking liquid has completely evaporated, about 10 minutes.

Add the wine and cook until the wine is reduced to 1 to 2 tablespoons and the shallots are very tender, about 5 minutes. Stir in the butter and serve.

❖ PARSNIP GRATIN

SERVES 6

4 cups heavy cream

6 parsnips, peeled and cut into ⅛-inch slices

¼ teaspoon freshly grated nutmeg

Salt and freshly ground black pepper, to taste

A side dish of earthy elegance for the Thanksgiving feast, this parsnip gratin from Tom Colicchio also goes well with roast lamb and chicken. It can be prepared early in the day and heated before serving.

Preheat the oven to 350°F. Bring the cream to a boil in a large heavy saucepan. Add the parsnips, and cook until almost tender, about 10 minutes. Remove the parsnips with a slotted spoon and arrange them in an even layer in a large gratin dish (or in 6 smaller dishes, if desired).

Add the nutmeg, salt, and pepper to the cream and simmer over medium heat until it is reduced by half. Pour the cream over the parsnips. Bake until golden brown on top, about 8 minutes.

❖ LEMON VEGETABLE COUSCOUS

SERVES 4 TO 6

2 carrots, cubed

2 tablespoons olive oil

1 red bell pepper, cored, seeded, and diced

1 zucchini, cubed

1 red onion, diced

1 teaspoon ground turmeric

Pinch saffron threads

Salt and freshly ground black pepper, to taste

2 cups chicken or vegetable broth, simmering

2 cups couscous

1 tablespoon chopped fresh parsley

1 tablespoon minced Preserved Lemons
(page 119), for garnish

*Matthew Kenney serves this flavorful couscous along with salads,
chutneys, and flatbreads at casual Meze parties (page 52).*

In a large pot of salted boiling water, blanch the carrots for 1 to 2 minutes. Remove and immediately refresh in cold water. Drain. Heat the olive oil in a large skillet over medium heat. Sauté the carrots, bell pepper, zucchini, and onion until the onion is translucent, about 5 minutes. Add the turmeric and cook for 1 minute. Add the saffron and season with salt and black pepper. Add the broth and stir to combine.

Place the couscous in a large bowl, pour the vegetable mixture over, and mix well with a fork. Cover with plastic wrap and let stand for 12 to 15 minutes, until all the liquid is absorbed. Fluff with a fork, garnish with the parsley and preserved lemon, and serve.

❖ SPINACH PURÉE IN PHYLLO

MAKES 12 PHYLLO PURSES

About ¹/₂ cup (1 stick) butter

1 onion, thinly sliced

2 pounds spinach, stems trimmed, washed well,
and dried

Salt and freshly ground black pepper, to taste

Six 12x18-inch sheets frozen phyllo dough,
thawed

3 tablespoons freshly grated Parmesan cheese

*These delicate-looking phyllo purses contain a rich spinach purée.
Daniel Boulud serves them with his Roasted Duck with Warm Cherries
(page 97), but you can serve them with any meat entrée.*

Heat 1 tablespoon of the butter in a small skillet over medium heat. Sauté the onion for 5 to 6 minutes, until soft. Transfer to a food processor and set aside.

In a large pot of salted boiling water, cook the spinach for 3 to 5 minutes, until tender. Drain well, pressing on the leaves to extract all the water. Transfer to the food processor with the onions.

In a small saucepan over medium heat, melt $2^{1}/_{2}$ tablespoons of the butter and cook until light brown. Add to the spinach and onions in the food processor and process until very smooth. Season with salt and pepper. Transfer the purée to a bowl and set aside.

Preheat the oven to 425°F. Melt the remaining butter in a small saucepan. Brush 1 sheet of phyllo with melted butter and sprinkle with $1^{1}/_{2}$ teaspoons of Parmesan. Place another sheet on top of the phyllo, brush with butter and sprinkle with Parmesan. Repeat with 1 more sheet of phyllo to make a stack of 3 sheets. Cut the stacked phyllo into six 6x6-inch squares. Repeat with the 3 remaining sheets. Spoon some of the spinach purée onto each square, bring up the corners, and twist closed to form a purse. Place the purses on a baking sheet and bake for 5 to 7 minutes, until lightly browned.

❖ NEAPOLITAN-STYLE EGGPLANT

SERVES 8

Eggplant:

6 thin eggplants, peeled and cut into $1^{1}/_{2}$-inch cubes

About $^{1}/_{2}$ cup coarse salt

About $1^{1}/_{2}$ cups all-purpose flour

2 cups vegetable oil

$^{1}/_{4}$ cup olive oil

Sauce:

$^{1}/_{2}$ cup olive oil

6 anchovy fillets packed in oil, drained

2 tablespoons red wine vinegar

Salt and freshly ground black pepper, to taste

$^{1}/_{4}$ cup finely chopped fresh flat-leaf parsley

2 garlic cloves, finely minced

Giuliano Bugialli tosses deep-fried eggplant in oil, vinegar, and anchovies for this Italian classic.

To prepare the eggplant, spread the cubes over a large platter and sprinkle the coarse salt over them. Let stand for 30 minutes. Rinse the eggplant under cold water, drain, and dry with paper towels.

Lightly flour the eggplant in batches by shaking the cubes with flour in a colander, so the excess flour falls through.

Heat the vegetable oil and olive oil in a deep fryer or deep skillet to 375°F. Fry the eggplant in batches, about 15 pieces at a time, turning them until they are golden brown all over. With a slotted spoon, transfer the cooked eggplant to a platter lined with paper towels, and keep warm.

To prepare the sauce, heat the olive oil in a small heavy saucepan over low heat. Add the anchovies and mash them with a fork into the oil. Add the vinegar, season with salt and pepper, and cook for 2 minutes.

Transfer the eggplant to a serving platter and pour the anchovy sauce over the top. Sprinkle with the parsley and garlic, toss well, and serve.

❖ SWISS CHARD TIMBALES

SERVES 8

2 pounds Swiss chard, trimmed and washed

¼ cup fresh lemon juice

½ teaspoon salt

8 ounces sliced bacon, cut into 1-inch matchsticks

2 tablespoons olive oil

2 leeks, white part only, julienned and well washed

4 shallots, finely minced

Leaves from 6 fresh thyme sprigs

1 cup plain nonfat yogurt

¼ cup freshly grated Parmesan cheese

2 large egg yolks

Salt and freshly ground black pepper, to taste

In these elegant timbales from Marjorie Reed Gordon, chard leaves are a beautiful wrapping for bacon, leeks, and chard stems in a yogurt-based custard. Gordon likes to serve them with Seared Three-Pepper Venison Chops with Three-Lily Jam (page 110).

Cut off the stems from the Swiss chard and cut into ¼-inch dice. Reserve the greens.

Bring 2 cups water, the lemon juice, and salt to a boil in a large saucepan. Add the chard stems and simmer for 10 minutes, or until tender. Drain and set aside.

In a large saucepan of salted boiling water, blanch the chard greens for 1 minute. Remove and immediately refresh in cold water. Drain, pat dry, and set aside.

Cook the bacon in a large skillet over medium-low heat until most of the fat is rendered. Do not allow the bacon to crisp. Pour off the fat and reduce the heat to low. Add the olive oil, leeks, shallots, and thyme and sauté for 5 to 6 minutes, until the shallots are translucent. Add the yogurt and simmer until it is reduced by half. Remove the pan from the heat and stir in the diced chard stems, the Parmesan, egg yolks, salt, and pepper.

Line eight 2-ounce ramekins or custard cups with aluminum foil. Then line the ramekins with the Swiss chard greens, allowing them to hang over all around the top of each. Fill with the bacon and chard mixture and fold the overhanging greens over the top. Cover with aluminum foil. (The timbales can be prepared to this point and refrigerated overnight. Bring to room temperature before steaming.)

Preheat the oven to 350°F. Place the ramekins in a 13x9-inch baking pan. Pour enough hot water into the pan to come halfway up the ramekins. Cover the pan with aluminum foil and bake for 15 minutes. Remove the ramekins from the pan and unmold each one onto a plate. Carefully remove the foil and serve.

❖ LEMON ASPARAGUS

SERVES 4

1 pound thin asparagus, trimmed
¼ cup white wine vinegar
¾ cup Lemon Oil (recipe follows)
Salt and freshly ground black pepper, to taste

For a slightly more intense lemon flavor, let the asparagus marinate for a few hours in the vinaigrette. Use the leftover lemon oil for zingy stir-fries or to enliven a tossed salad.

Bring 2 inches of water to a boil in a large skillet. Blanch the asparagus for 2 minutes, drain, and immediately refresh in cold water. Drain.

Combine the vinegar and lemon oil in a large shallow serving bowl. Add the asparagus, season with salt and pepper, and toss. Serve.

LEMON OIL

MAKES 2 CUPS

Zest of 3 large lemons, removed with a vegetable peeler
2 cups olive oil

Place the zest and ¼ cup of the olive oil in a mortar. Pound and rub the zest with a pestle for 1 minute to release the citrus oil. Transfer the mixture to a clean glass jar and add the remaining 1¾ cups olive oil. Cover and allow to steep for 4 days at room temperature.

Strain the oil into a clean glass jar, cover, and store at room temperature for up to 1 week.

❖ STUFFED SUMMER SQUASH

SERVES 4

2 small yellow summer squash
2 tablespoons olive oil
1 onion, chopped
1 red bell pepper, cored, seeded, and chopped
1 green bell pepper, cored, seeded, and chopped
2 garlic cloves, minced
3 tablespoons freshly grated Parmesan cheese
2 tablespoons chopped fresh parsley
1 tablespoon chopped fresh basil
1 teaspoon chopped fresh oregano
Salt and freshly ground black pepper, to taste

This high-summer combination of red and green bell peppers, garlic, and onion comes from the Outermost Inn. It can be made ahead and served warm or cold.

Cut the squash lengthwise in half. Scoop out the flesh, leaving a ½-inch shell, and dice the flesh. Reserve the squash halves.

Heat the olive oil in a large skillet over medium heat. Sauté the diced squash, onion, red and green peppers, and garlic for 8 to 10 minutes, until tender. Transfer to a large bowl and stir in the Parmesan, parsley, basil, and oregano. Season with salt and pepper.

Preheat the oven to 350°F. In a vegetable steamer or a colander set over boiling water, steam the squash halves for 5 minutes. Place on a baking sheet and stuff with the vegetable mixture. Bake for 10 minutes, until the squash halves are tender. Serve warm.

Winter Fantasy

For Michael Trapp, entertaining is a chance to pull out all the creative stops. An antiques dealer known for his fantasy parties, Trapp loves to lavish his imagination on his guests — "It's worth going the extra mile" is the way he explains it. One December, he created a veritable forest inside his Connecticut home by recycling deadfall boughs into romantic decorations. Guests gathered in the garden room, a former garage, where the host had decked the walls with branches of white pine using hammer and nails. Moss, scattered with vibrant radishes and plump fennel bulbs, became a festive runner for the stone table laden with appetizers. Tiered Victorian glass cake stands piled high with assortments of shiny fruits and vegetables doubled as Christmas trees. Candles in the crystal chandelier flickered like stars.

On the dining table — a honed marble slab from a Dutch candy factory — foxgloves, snow-white amaryllis, anemonies, and tulips were set in Venetian glass vases. Glass pitchers, silver julep cups, and Biedermeier wine glasses added to the glittering ensemble. Whimsical place mats of florist's moss showed off creamware and old silver.

Like the food he prepares, the atmosphere Trapp creates is "temporary, like a dream. It's beautiful, then it's gone as quickly as it came." And his guests can't wait until the next magical event.

Casual Hospitality

Improvisation is Marie-Paule Pellé's forte. A Parisian interior designer known for her skill in pulling together a room, a film set, or a new apartment in record time, she approaches entertaining with the same panache. Her secret for spur-of-the-moment parties: "Be organized and fast." She can arrange a dinner party in as little as half an hour — angst-free.

Guests gather in a tiny, leafy garden off the kitchen. Champagne and biscuits are served on a table dressed with an antique organdy cloth and a Napoleonic compote.

When dinner is ready, everyone moves to the kitchen, where Pellé squeezes as many as twelve around a simple country table covered with an African batik. Her philosophy is that guests enjoy themselves more when they're elbow to elbow.

Dinner often starts with store-bought brioche filled with truffle-scented scrambled eggs. The main course might be poached salmon, followed by goat cheese spiffed up with a quick coating of finely chopped hazelnuts. Dessert is likely to be fresh berries, poached peaches, and ice cream. It's all simple French fare, but in Pellé's capable hands it seems like a million francs.

4

SWEET ENDINGS

Sinful, luscious, refreshing, irresistible — dessert is for many of us the most exciting part of the meal. It can be a simple bowl of raspberries or a beautiful poached pear. It can be a comforting fruit clafouti, crisp, or pie. It can be elaborate — a dark chocolate soufflé or white chocolate mousse. It should always be a delight to the eye.

At informal parties, desserts might be put on the table for guests to help themselves. If there is room, dessert plates and any extra sauces can be set up ahead of time on a sideboard or table. A fragile dish like ice cream, sorbet, or a soufflé should be brought straight to the table and served there. Fruit and cheese might be served with port or another dessert wine.

This is a time for leisurely conversation, and depending on the mood, the setting, and the host, guests might stay around the table for coffee or retire to another room. Coffee should include decaffeinated as well as regular; herbal tea and sparkling water are thoughtful additional offerings. Cognac, a sparkling wine, or Champagne can provide an elegant ending to any dinner.

Desserts

❖ STRAWBERRY SHORTCAKE WITH HOT CREAM SAUCE

SERVES 6

Shortcake:

2 cups all-purpose flour

¼ cup sugar

1½ teaspoons baking powder

¼ teaspoon freshly grated nutmeg

¼ teaspoon salt

½ cup (1 stick) unsalted butter at room
    temperature

1 large egg, lightly beaten

About ¾ cup half-and-half

Sauce:

2 cups heavy cream

¼ cup sugar

¼ cup (½ stick) unsalted butter

2 pints strawberries, hulled and halved

Fresh mint leaves, for garnish

Legend has it that this shortcake sauce so intrigued Julia Child that it sent her running into the Boonville Hotel kitchen to unearth its secret. What she discovered was a rich sauce of cream, butter, and sugar, simmered until thickened.

To prepare the shortcake, preheat the oven to 400°F. In a large bowl, mix together the flour, sugar, baking powder, nutmeg, and salt. Add the butter and blend with a pastry blender or your fingers until the mixture resembles coarse cornmeal.

Place the egg in a 1-cup measure and add enough half-and-half to make 1 cup. Slowly add to the flour mixture, stirring with a fork. Do not overwork the dough. With a spoon, drop the dough onto an ungreased baking sheet in 6 equal mounds. Bake for 10 to 12 minutes.

To prepare the sauce, in a large saucepan over low heat, combine the cream, sugar, and butter. Bring to a simmer and cook gently, stirring frequently, for about 30 minutes, until thick. Watch carefully, as the mixture tends to boil over very quickly.

Split the hot shortcakes in half. Place the bottom halves on 6 plates and top with the strawberries and the shortcake tops. Ladle the sauce on top, garnish with mint leaves, and serve.

❖ STRAWBERRIES WITH MASCARPONE

MAKES 20 STRAWBERRIES

20 large long-stemmed strawberries

8 ounces mascarpone cheese

⅓ cup superfine sugar

½ teaspoon ground cinnamon

1 tablespoon crushed pistachio nuts

Pass these strawberries stuffed with creamy mascarpone on a tray at a cocktail reception or offer them as part of a buffet.

Cut the strawberries lengthwise in half, just to the side of the stems, without damaging the leaves and leaving one half of each with the stem intact. Reserve the pieces without stems for another use.

Combine the mascarpone, sugar, and cinnamon and stir until creamy. Transfer to a pastry bag fitted with a star tip and pipe a star onto each strawberry half. Sprinkle with the pistachios and serve.

❖POACHED PEARS WITH BRANDY AND GINGER

SERVES 6

2 cups dry white wine

1 cup sugar

2 cinnamon sticks

One 1-inch piece fresh ginger, peeled and sliced

6 barely ripe pears, peeled and cored from the
    bottom, stems left intact

6 lemon slices

1 tablespoon brandy

Poached pears make a scrumptious dessert to serve at parties. These, poached in a wine and ginger syrup, come from the Soutine bakery in New York. Look for beautiful specimens of Bosc, Comice, or Anjou.

In a 2-quart saucepan over medium heat, combine the wine, sugar, cinnamon, and ginger and cook, stirring, until the sugar is dissolved, about 3 minutes. Add the pears and simmer gently for about 25 minutes, until just tender. If the liquid does not cover the pears, turn them occasionally during cooking to make sure they cook evenly. Remove the saucepan from the heat and let the pears to cool in the syrup. Transfer the pears to a serving dish.

Place the saucepan with the syrup over high heat, add the lemon slices, and bring to a boil. Continue to boil until the syrup is thickened and reduced by half, about 15 minutes. Strain through a fine strainer into a small bowl, reserving the lemon slices. Add the brandy to the syrup, stir, and let cool. Spoon the syrup over pears, garnish with the reserved lemon slices, and serve.

❖ CHOCOLATE PEARS

SERVES 6

1 cup sugar

4 cups water

Juice of 1 lemon

2 cinnamon sticks

4 cloves

6 firm Anjou or Comice pears, stems left intact

4 ounces unsweetened chocolate, broken into small pieces

2 ounces semisweet chocolate, broken into small pieces

½ cup (1 stick) unsalted butter

Fresh mint sprigs, for garnish

Spectacular to look at, these poached pears dipped in chocolate are easy to make. This was a popular dessert in the 1970s, when the late Maurice Moore-Betty included it in his cooking classes.

In a large saucepan over medium heat, combine the sugar and water and cook, stirring, for about 3 minutes, until the sugar has dissolved. Stir in the lemon juice, cinnamon, and cloves and simmer, covered, for 10 to 15 minutes.

Peel the pears and trim the bottoms so that they stand upright. Place the pears in the syrup and poach until tender, 30 to 40 minutes, depending on the ripeness of the pears (test with a toothpick). Allow the pears to cool in the syrup, then chill thoroughly, preferably overnight.

Place both chocolates in the top of double boiler set over simmering water. Add the butter and stir until melted and smooth. Remove from the heat.

Remove the pears from the syrup and gently pat dry. Dip the pears into the melted chocolate and coat evenly, using a spoon if necessary. Lift the pears to drain off the excess chocolate. Arrange on a serving dish and garnish with mint. (The pears will keep in the refrigerator for up to 36 hours. Allow to come to room temperature before serving.)

APRICOT AND CHERRY CLAFOUTI

SERVES 6 TO 8

3 large eggs

I cup heavy cream

²/₃ cup all-purpose flour

6 tablespoons unsalted butter, melted,
    plus ¹/₄ cup (¹/₂ stick) solid

I teaspoon vanilla extract

¹/₂ teaspoon salt

5 cups pitted and halved apricots

¹/₂ cup pitted and halved cherries

¹/₂ cup sugar

2 to 3 tablespoons brandy or Amaretto

¹/₈ teaspoon ground cinnamon mixed with
    2 teaspoons sugar

¹/₄ cup maple syrup

Vanilla ice cream, for serving

A clafouti is a simple French country dessert of batter and fruit, usually cherries. This version adds fresh apricots for a little bit of bite.

Preheat the oven to 375°F. In a blender, combine the eggs, cream, flour, melted butter, vanilla, and salt and process for 1 minute. Set aside.

Melt the remaining ¹/₄ cup butter in a large nonstick skillet over medium heat. Add the apricots, cherries, sugar, and brandy and sauté for 2 to 3 minutes, until the fruit is hot.

Meanwhile, butter a 10-inch pie plate and heat in the oven for 5 minutes. With a slotted spoon, transfer the hot fruit to the pie plate, reserving the juices in the skillet. Pour the egg mixture over the fruit, sprinkle with the cinnamon sugar, and bake for 25 to 30 minutes, until just set.

Meanwhile, in a small pan over low heat, combine the maple syrup with ¹/₄ cup of the reserved fruit juices. Cook until heated through.

Cut the clafouti into wedges, transfer to dessert plates, and drizzle each with a spoonful or two of the warm sauce. Serve with vanilla ice cream.

AMBROSIA

SERVES 8

4 large Valencia or navel oranges

I cup pecans, coarsely chopped

I cup shredded unsweetened coconut

Ambrosia it's called, and food of the gods it is — a lively combination of oranges, pecans, and shredded coconut. This old Southern recipe from Olga Ellis has long been part of many Thanksgiving celebrations.

Working over a bowl to catch the juice, peel the oranges, removing all the pith. With a sharp knife, slice the orange sections from the membranes.

In a large serving bowl, combine the oranges with their juice, pecans, and coconut. Cover with plastic wrap and refrigerate until ready to serve.

Serving Cheese

Cheese as a separate course is gaining popularity in restaurants and at home. Whether offered before dessert as the French do, or after in the English style, pick just two or three perfectly ripe cheeses and arrange them attractively on a board or platter. The only support they need is a nub of crusty bread and a glass of wine.

Steven Jenkins, America's foremost authority on cheese, offers these ideas for including cheeses and their natural partners — nuts, dried and fresh fruit, chutneys and relishes — in almost every kind of entertaining.

Little "buttons" of goat cheese (above) can be zipped up with pink peppercorns, thyme, and extra virgin olive oil and served with bread or set atop a salad. They can also be splashed with honey or raspberry vinegar, and, for dessert, topped with plain yogurt and fresh fruit.

For a first course, nothing could be simpler than thin shards of Parmigiano-Reggiano — maybe the greatest cheese of all — sprinkled with balsamic vinegar, black pepper, and a few ripe figs (right).

For a sophisticated take on the traditional British ploughman's pub lunch (opposite), three of England's great country cheeses — Appleby Cheshire, Colston Bassett Stilton, and Keen's Cheddar — are served with walnuts and banana chutney instead of the traditional mango. With a chewy whole-grain bread and a glass of red wine or port, this makes an exquisite lunch or cheese course at dinner.

❖ LEMON RICOTTA HOTCAKES

MAKES ABOUT TWELVE 5-INCH PANCAKES

6 large eggs, separated

1 1/2 cups ricotta cheese

1/2 cup (1 stick) butter, melted and cooled

1/2 cup all-purpose flour

1/4 cup granulated sugar

2 tablespoons grated lemon zest, plus more
for garnish

1/2 teaspoon salt

Confectioners' sugar, for garnish

1 cup blackberries, for garnish (optional)

*Although these delectable hotcakes are served for breakfast at the
Four Seasons Hotel in New York, their creator, chef Susan
Weaver, believes they make a good dessert, too. Serve them with fresh
berries, maple syrup, and perhaps a little whipped cream.*

In a large bowl, combine the egg yolks, ricotta, and butter. In another bowl, combine the flour, granulated sugar, lemon zest, and salt. Gradually beat in the egg mixture. Set aside.

In a small bowl with an electric mixer, beat the egg whites until firm peaks form. Carefully fold the egg whites into the batter.

Lightly grease a griddle or nonstick pan and place over medium heat for 1 minute. With a 1/4-cup measuring cup, ladle the batter onto the griddle to make 3 or 4 hotcakes. Cook the hotcakes for 2 to 3 minutes, until bubbles begin to appear on the top. Turn the hotcakes and cook for 2 to 3 minutes more, until golden on the bottom. Stack the hotcakes on an ovenproof dish and keep warm in a low oven while cooking the remaining cakes. Garnish with a sprinkling of confectioners' sugar, lemon zest, and blackberries, if using, and serve.

❖ POUND CAKE WITH LEMON GLAZE

SERVES 12

Glaze:

1/3 cup fresh lemon juice

1/2 cup sugar

1 tablespoon unsalted butter

Pinch salt

Cake:

1 cup (2 sticks) cold unsalted butter

1 2/3 cups sugar

1/4 teaspoon salt

5 large eggs

2 1/4 cups sifted cake flour

1 tablespoon vanilla extract

1 teaspoon fresh lemon juice

*A pound cake in the pantry is, according to Edna Lewis, the
perfect standby in case company should arrive unexpectedly. This one, with
its lemony glaze, can be kept fresh for several days.*

To prepare the glaze, in a small saucepan over medium heat, combine the lemon juice, sugar, butter, and salt. Simmer for 1 minute. Remove from the heat, cover with waxed paper, and let cool.

To prepare the cake, butter and lightly flour a 9-inch tube pan, preferably with a removable bottom. In a large bowl, beat the butter with a wooden spoon until it becomes shiny, about 5 minutes. Add the sugar and salt and beat until well mixed. Then stir in a circular motion until the sugar dissolves and the mixture is no longer grainy, about 10 to 15 minutes.

Add 3 of the eggs, one at a time, stirring well after each addition. Add 2 tablespoons of the flour and stir well (the flour keeps the batter from separating). Add the remaining 2 eggs, stirring well. Add the remaining flour in 4 parts, stirring well after each addition. Beat in the vanilla and lemon juice.

Spoon the batter into the prepared pan. Place the pan in a cold oven and turn the oven heat to 225°F. After 20 minutes, raise the heat to 325°F. Continue to bake for about 40 minutes more, or until a cake tester inserted in the center of the cake comes out clean.

Run a knife around the inside of the pan and immediately turn the cake out onto a wire rack. Spoon the glaze over the warm cake and let cool. (The cake can be stored in an airtight container for up to 2 days.) Cut into slices and serve.

❖ LEMON ALMOND POUND CAKE

SERVES 6 TO 8

5 tablespoons butter

1/3 cup olive oil

3/4 cup granulated sugar

12 ounces almond paste

Grated zest of 3 lemons

5 large eggs

1/2 cup cake flour

1 teaspoon baking powder

3 tablespoons lemon liqueur

Confectioners' sugar, for garnish

Almond paste makes this lemony pound cake moist and rich. The idea belongs to Matthew Kenney of Matthew's in New York City.

Preheat the oven to 325°F. Butter a 9-inch round cake pan. Line the bottom with parchment paper, butter the paper, and dust with flour. In a medium bowl with an electric mixer, beat together the butter, olive oil, and granulated sugar until fluffy. Add the almond paste and lemon zest and beat until smooth. Beat in the eggs, one at a time, beating well after each addition. Fold in the flour and baking powder.

Pour the batter into the prepared pan and bake for about 1 hour, until a cake tester inserted in the center of the cake comes out almost clean. Let cool. Transfer the cake to a serving plate. Brush the lemon liqueur over the top and sprinkle with confectioners' sugar. Cut into wedges and serve.

❖ RUSTIC APPLE TART

SERVES 6 TO 8

Pastry:

1 cup all-purpose flour

1 teaspoon granulated sugar

$^1\!/_2$ teaspoon salt

$^1\!/_2$ teaspoon baking powder

3 tablespoons cold unsalted butter, cut into $^1\!/_2$-inch bits

$^1\!/_4$ cup sour cream

$^1\!/_2$ teaspoon white wine vinegar or cider vinegar, mixed with 1$^1\!/_2$ teaspoons ice water

Filling:

1$^1\!/_2$ pounds apples, such as McIntosh or Winesap

2 tablespoons fresh lemon juice

$^1\!/_4$ cup granulated sugar

$^3\!/_4$ teaspoon ground cinnamon

2 tablespoons all-purpose flour

1 teaspoon unsalted butter

2 teaspoons confectioners' sugar

For many cooks, a free-form pastry shell is much easier to make than a perfect crust in a tart tin. It's much quicker and in many ways more attractive, too.

To prepare the pastry, combine the flour, granulated sugar, salt, and baking powder in a medium bowl. Add the butter and cut it into the flour with a pastry cutter or two knives until it makes a very coarse meal. Place the bowl in the freezer for about 5 minutes; this will firm up the butter and insure a flakier crust.

Add the sour cream and vinegar mixture to the bowl and quickly blend it into the flour with a pastry cutter or fork. Squeeze the dough 7 or 8 times with your hands to incorporate the loose bits and gather the dough together into a rough ball. If the dough is very dry and does not hold together, add a little more ice water, one teaspoon at a time. Flatten the dough into a 1-inch-thick disk, wrap in plastic, and refrigerate for at least 30 minutes.

Remove the dough from the refrigerator and let it sit at room temperature for about 15 minutes. On a lightly floured surface, roll the dough into a 14- to 15-inch circle. Transfer the dough to a baking sheet and refrigerate while you prepare the apple filling.

Preheat the oven to 400°F. Peel and core the apples. Slice them into $^1\!/_4$-inch slices. You should have about 3 cups of fruit. In a bowl, toss the apples with the lemon juice, 3 tablespoons of the granulated sugar, and the cinnamon. In a small bowl, combine the flour with the remaining 1 tablespoon granulated sugar.

Sprinkle the flour mixture over the dough, leaving a 2-inch border uncovered. Arrange the apple slices evenly over the flour mixture. Fold the 2-inch border of dough over the apples in overlapping folds to form the sides of the tart. Brush the folds of dough lightly with water and crimp with your fingers to seal the folds. Dot the apples with the butter.

Bake the tart for about 40 minutes, covering the crust with foil after 20 minutes if it is browning too rapidly. The tart should be golden brown and the apples tender, with syrupy juices. Let cool for 10 minutes.

Slide the tart onto a serving platter, sift the confectioners' sugar evenly over the crust, and serve.

❖ APRICOT TART

SERVES 8

Pastry cream:

2 cups half-and-half

1 vanilla bean, split

5 large egg yolks

$\frac{1}{2}$ cup sugar

$\frac{1}{4}$ cup all-purpose flour

1 sheet ($\frac{1}{2}$ pound) frozen puff pastry, thawed

1 large egg, beaten with 1 tablespoon water

$\frac{1}{2}$ cup apricot jam, pressed through a sieve

$\frac{1}{3}$ cup red currant jelly

3 tablespoons sugar

2 teaspoons water or rum

12 canned pitted apricot halves, marinated in 2 tablespoons rum for 30 minutes and drained

2 cups raspberries

Janet Fanto's apricot tart is one of Michael Trapp's favorites and is served at his holiday parties. The pastry cream can be made up to two days in advance, and the tart up to one day.

To prepare the pastry cream, in a saucepan over low heat, heat the half-and-half with the vanilla bean until small bubbles begin to appear around the edge. Remove the bean and scrape the seeds from the bean into the half-and-half. Set aside.

In a medium saucepan, whisk the egg yolks and sugar together until thick and lemon colored. Gradually sift the flour over the egg mixture and mix until well combined. Slowly stir in the half-and-half. Place the pan over very low heat and cook, stirring constantly, until the mixture heavily coats the back of a spoon, about 15 minutes. Pour the pastry cream into a bowl and cool, stirring a few times. (The pastry cream can be prepared up to 2 days in advance. Place a piece of waxed paper on the surface and refrigerate.)

To prepare the tart, preheat the oven to 350°F. On a lightly floured surface, roll out the puff pastry to a 14x11-inch rectangle. Cut two 1-inch-wide strips from each side of the rectangle. Transfer the rectangle to an ungreased baking sheet and prick with a fork. Brush evenly with the egg mixture. Place one pastry strip on each edge of the dough to make a border, aligning the edges and trimming the ends as necessary. Brush the top of the strips with the egg mixture. Place the remaining pastry strips on top of the first ones, trimming them as necessary, and brush with the egg mixture.

Bake for 20 minutes, until the pastry is golden. Check the pastry after 5 minutes; if the bottom is puffed, remove from the oven, prick all over with a fork, and continue baking. Let cool.

In a small saucepan over medium heat, combine the apricot jam, currant jelly, sugar, and water. Bring to a boil, stirring constantly. Cook until thick, about 2 minutes. Cool for 5 minutes.

Fill the cooled pastry shell with the pastry cream. Top with the apricots and raspberries, and brush the glaze on top of the fruit. Chill until ready to serve.

❖ PECAN PIE

SERVES 6 TO 8

1 cup sugar

1 cup dark corn syrup

¹/₂ cup (1 stick) butter or margarine

4 large eggs, at room temperature

1 teaspoon vanilla extract

1 cup chopped pecans, plus 1 cup pecan halves

One 9-inch unbaked pie shell

The extra handful of pecans, added at the end, makes this pie delightfully nutty. Made with either a prepared pastry shell or a homemade one, it can be prepared a day ahead and warmed up.

Preheat the oven to 400°F. In a saucepan over medium heat, combine the sugar, corn syrup, and butter. Bring to a boil, remove from the heat, and set aside.

In a large bowl with an electric mixer, beat the eggs until foamy. While beating, add the syrup mixture in a steady stream. Stir in the vanilla and chopped pecans. Pour the filling into the pie shell. Sprinkle the top with the pecan halves and place the pie on a baking sheet. Bake for 35 to 40 minutes. Cool on a rack and serve.

❖ JAMES BEARD'S PUMPKIN PIE WITH CANDIED GINGER

MAKES TWO 9-INCH PIES;
EACH PIE SERVES 6 TO 8

Two 9-inch unbaked pie shells

2 cups canned unsweetened pumpkin

6 large eggs, lightly beaten

2 cups heavy cream

²/₃ cup sugar

¹/₂ cup finely chopped candied ginger, plus slivered candied ginger, for garnish

¹/₂ cup Cognac

1 teaspoon ground cinnamon

¹/₄ teaspoon freshly grated nutmeg

¹/₄ teaspoon ground cloves

¹/₄ teaspoon salt

Sweetened whipped cream, for serving

The addition of crystallized ginger gives this creamy pie its sophisticated taste. The recipe is based on one from James Beard.

Preheat the oven to 425°F. Line the pie shells with foil and fill with pie weights or dried beans. Bake for 12 minutes. Remove the foil and pie weights. Reduce the oven temperature to 375°F.

Place the pumpkin in a bowl and make a well in the center. Add the eggs, cream, sugar, chopped ginger, Cognac, cinnamon, nutmeg, cloves, and salt to the center of the well and blend thoroughly with a wooden spoon. Taste to correct the seasoning.

Divide the mixture evenly between the two pie shells and bake for 35 to 40 minutes, until a knife inserted in the center comes out clean. Transfer to wire racks and let cool. Cut each pie into wedges, garnish with slivered ginger, and serve with whipped cream.

Clockwise from left: Pecan Pie, Ambrosia (page 139), James Beard's Pumpkin Pie with Candied Ginger.

❖ MAPLE WALNUT TART

SERVES 6 TO 8

Dough:

¹/₂ cup granulated sugar

1 cup all-purpose flour

¹/₂ cup (1 stick) cold butter, cut into
¹/₂-inch pieces

1 large egg yolk

1 tablespoon cold water

Filling:

¹/₃ cup maple syrup

2 tablespoons light corn syrup

1 tablespoon maple sugar

1¹/₂ teaspoons cake flour

2 large eggs

¹/₄ teaspoon vanilla extract

¹/₈ teaspoon salt

1¹/₂ tablespoons butter, melted

³/₄ cup walnuts, chopped

This lush walnut tart, laced with rich maple syrup, is served for Thanksgiving dessert at the Mayflower Inn in Washington, Connecticut. Served à la mode, it's a delightful ending to a grand meal. Maple sugar is available at gourmet food stores.

To prepare the dough, in a food processor, combine the sugar and all-purpose flour. Pulse to combine. Add the butter and pulse until the mixture resembles coarse cornmeal. Add the egg yolk and water and pulse until the dough just begins to clump together. Shape the dough into a ball, wrap the dough in plastic wrap, and refrigerate for 1 hour.

Preheat the oven to 350°F. Place the dough on a lightly floured surface and knead briefly until soft. Roll the dough into an 11-inch round. Line a 9-inch fluted tart pan, preferably one with a removable bottom, with the dough. Trim the excess and prick the dough all over with a fork. Bake for 12 minutes. Set aside.

To prepare the filling, combine the maple syrup, corn syrup, maple sugar, and cake flour in a medium bowl. Mix well and set aside.

In another medium bowl, beat together the eggs, vanilla, and salt until foamy, about 2 minutes. Gradually beat in the melted butter, mixing well. Add half of the maple mixture and beat to incorporate. Add the remaining maple mixture and continue beating until well combined.

Spread the walnuts evenly over the bottom of the pastry shell, then pour maple filling over walnuts. Bake for 20 minutes, until golden brown.

❖ NOVEMBER PUDDING

SERVES 10

2 cups sifted all-purpose flour

1 teaspoon baking soda

1 cup (2 sticks) unsalted butter at room
temperature

1 cup packed light brown sugar

4 large eggs, lightly beaten

4 heaping tablespoons raspberry jam

3 fresh or canned apricots, halved and pitted

Apricot Sauce (recipe follows)

*This spicy, steamed, cakelike pudding, courtesy of
Maurice Moore-Betty, can be made hours ahead of time and
reheated. It is served with a luscious apricot sauce.*

Sift the flour and baking soda together into a bowl. Set aside. In a large bowl with an electric mixer, cream the butter until fluffy. Gradually beat in the sugar, eggs, and raspberry jam until well mixed (the mixture will look curdled). Sift the flour mixture over the creamed mixture, a little at a time, and fold in thoroughly.

Lightly butter a 2-quart pudding mold. Pour the batter into the mold and cover with a tight-fitting lid (or seal tightly with heavy-duty aluminum foil). Place the mold in a large pot and add enough boiling water to come two thirds of the way up the mold. Cover the pot tightly and steam over low heat for 2 hours; add more boiling water as necessary.

Remove the mold from the pan and let rest for 5 minutes. Unmold the hot pudding onto a serving plate and top with the apricot halves. Serve hot or at room temperature with the apricot sauce.

APRICOT SAUCE

MAKES ABOUT 1 1/2 CUPS

One 12-ounce jar apricot jam

1/2 cup sugar

1/2 cup water

1 to 2 tablespoons Grand Marnier, Cognac, or kirsch

Combine the jam, sugar, and water in a saucepan over medium heat and cook, stirring constantly, for 5 minutes. Strain the sauce through a fine strainer into a bowl. Stir in the Grand Marnier.

❖ CHOCOLATE TART

SERVES 8 TO 10

Tart shell:

2¹/₂ cups all-purpose flour

1 cup plus 2 tablespoons confectioners' sugar

¹/₂ cup (1 stick) unsalted butter, cold

1 large egg

About 2 tablespoons ice water

Filling:

1 pound bittersweet chocolate, preferably
  Valrhona, broken into small pieces

1¹/₄ cups (2¹/₂ sticks) plus 1 tablespoon
  unsalted butter

3 large eggs

6 large egg yolks

7¹/₂ tablespoons sugar

New York chef Jean-Georges Vongerichten serves this intense chocolate tart, warm and slightly runny, with wedges of orange and grapefruit. The crisp pâté sucrée shell holds the chocolate.

To prepare the tart shell, in a food processor fitted with the plastic blade, combine the flour, sugar, and butter. Process until the mixture resembles oatmeal. Add the egg and process until blended. With the motor running, slowly add the ice water, a tablespoon at a time, until the mixture just forms a ball.

Lightly flour a work surface. Put the dough on the work surface and, using the heel of your hand, break off and smear bits of pastry across the surface to ensure that the ingredients are well blended. Shape the dough into a flat round and wrap in plastic. Refrigerate for 1 hour.

Preheat the oven to 375°F. Lightly flour both sides of the dough and place between 2 pieces of waxed paper. Roll the dough out to a round about ¹/₄-inch thick. Carefully fit it into a 9-inch fluted tart pan, preferably one with a removable bottom. Trim the excess dough. Refrigerate for 10 minutes.

Line the pastry with aluminum foil and fill with pie weights or dried beans. Bake for 5 to 6 minutes. Remove the weights and foil, prick the bottom with a fork, and continue baking for 8 to 10 minutes more, until the tart shell is pale brown and has slightly withdrawn from the side of the pan.

To prepare the filling, reduce the oven temperature to 350°F. Melt the chocolate and butter in the top of a double boiler set over simmering water, stirring until smooth. Remove from the heat.

In a large bowl with an electric mixer, beat the eggs and egg yolks until foamy. Add the sugar and beat until pale and lemon-colored. Add the melted chocolate mixture and stir until thick and shiny. Pour into the tart shell and bake for 15 minutes.

Let rest for 10 minutes (the filling will be slightly runny) before cutting into wedges. Serve.

❖ CHOCOLATE BREAD PUDDING

SERVES 6

One 12-inch-long brioche loaf, cut into 12 slices

1 cup (2 sticks) butter, melted

8 ounces bittersweet chocolate, broken into
    small pieces

3 cups heavy cream

1 cup milk

1 cup sugar

12 large egg yolks

1 teaspoon vanilla extract

Pinch salt

Old-fashioned bread pudding, the quintessential comfort dessert, has been making a comeback. For this rich, sinful version from Anne Rosenzweig, use the best chocolate you can find. You can substitute challah or any other kind of eggy yeast bread for the brioche.

Preheat the oven to 300°F. Put the bread slices on a baking sheet, brush with the butter, and toast in the oven until golden brown, about 10 minutes. Set aside.

Melt the chocolate in the top of a double boiler set over simmering water, stirring until smooth. Remove from the heat.

In a small heavy saucepan over medium heat, bring the cream and milk almost to a boil.

Meanwhile in a large bowl with an electric mixer, beat together the sugar and egg yolks until well blended. Slowly beat in the hot cream mixture. Beat in the melted chocolate. Strain through a fine strainer and skim off any foam. Stir in the vanilla and salt.

In a 9x12-inch baking dish, arrange the toasted bread in 2 rows, overlapping the slices as necessary. Pour the chocolate mixture over the bread. Cover with plastic wrap and weigh down with cans or other heavy weights. Let stand 1 hour, until the bread is soaked through.

Raise the oven temperature to 325°F. Remove the weights and plastic wrap from the baking dish and cover with aluminum foil. Punch about ten holes in the aluminum foil to allow the steam to escape. Set the baking dish in a larger roasting pan and pour in enough hot water to come halfway up the sides of the baking dish. Bake for 1 hour and 45 minutes, until the liquid has been absorbed and the pudding has a glossy look. Cut into squares and serve warm.

❖ CHOCOLATE SOUFFLÉS

SERVES 6

10 ounces semisweet chocolate, chopped

1 cup heavy cream

5 tablespoons superfine sugar

2 tablespoons unsalted butter

1 tablespoon dark rum

1 tablespoon vanilla extract

½ teaspoon salt

6 large egg yolks

9 large egg whites at room temperature

Pinch cream of tartar

Confectioners' sugar, for dusting

The hot chocolate soufflés served at Etats Unis restaurant have been rated the best in New York. Moist in the center and perfectly puffy, they make a spectacular end to a party meal.

Preheat the oven to 350°F. Butter six 4x2½-inch ramekins and sprinkle with sugar. In a saucepan over low heat, melt the chocolate with the cream, superfine sugar, butter, rum, vanilla, and salt, stirring until smooth. Remove from the heat and let cool slightly.

Stir the egg yolks into the chocolate mixture, one at a time, stirring well after each addition.

In a large bowl with an electric mixer, beat the egg whites with the cream of tartar until soft peaks form. Carefully fold the whites into the chocolate mixture. Divide the mixture among the prepared ramekins. Bake for 20 minutes. The soufflés will rise, but the centers should remain creamy. Dust with confectioners' sugar and serve immediately.

Outdoor Entertaining

One of the great pleasures of summer is an outdoor gathering with friends — a picnic lunch, backyard barbecue, candlelit supper on the patio. Whatever the occasion, setting the stage can be as much fun as the party itself. Chinese grass mats or rag rugs on the lawn are an easy way to create extra party space. The old Southern custom of rolling out oriental rugs on the grass and stacking cushions on them for seating provides a truly luxurious effect. Old garden furniture or benches with cotton cushions are never out of place.

The table itself can be a rustic board or a door on sawhorses if more "formal" outdoor furniture is not available; a tablecloth — from linen to gingham to sheeting — will give any table a finished look. Bright pottery and earthenware, colorful cotton napkins, jam jars full of wildflowers, jugs of flowering herbs and grasses, simple bistro glasses, inexpensive enamel plates and plastic-handled cutlery will keep things lighthearted and casual. The bar can be as simple as pitchers of soft drinks, ice tea, water, wine, or san-

gria and glasses on a tray. A more elaborate bar can have the makings of mixed drinks, with wine nearby on ice. Plates, napkins, glasses, and food can be ferried from the house in baskets, which are useful for cleanup afterward. Citronella candles and little wooden fans will keep everyone happy on even the hottest summer day.

Next to a barbecue, the easiest type of outdoor menu is one in which everything is served at room temper-

ature — salads, vegetables, meats, or fish, most of which can be made ahead of time. Pitchers of cold gazpacho or other cold soup make a nice beginning, and salads can be dressed at the table. Before-dinner nibbles — olives, cherry tomatoes, vegetable crudités, summer fruits — are perfect warm-weather appetizers. Platters on the table family-style keep the occasion easy and relaxed — which is, after all, what summer is all about.

On Provençal pottery and a checked cloth, a summer lunch awaits Paris decorator Jacques Grange's friends outside his farmhouse (opposite). For a California party, freshly squeezed lemonade and beer in hand-painted pilsner glasses are ready for guests (right).

Dining with a view: The city at night provides a shimmering backdrop for supper on the terrace (left). Flickering votive candles provide the table's romantic light.

On the ocean, a tawny umbrella shields diners from the sun (below). A basket of bottles, a vase of herbs, and a half wheel of cheese make for a simple, appealing picnic table.

On her deck overlooking a Long Island bay, restaurateur Barbara Smith sets out a summer lunch in nautical blue and white (opposite).

❖COLD CHOCOLATE SOUFFLÉ

SERVES 6 TO 8

1 envelope unflavored gelatin

3 tablespoons water

2 ounces unsweetened chocolate, broken
    into small pieces

1/2 cup confectioners' sugar

1 cup milk

3/4 cup granulated sugar

1 teaspoon vanilla extract

1/4 teaspoon salt

2 cups heavy cream

One 2-ounce block of bittersweet chocolate at
    room temperature

One of House Beautiful's favorite desserts over the years, this cold soufflé is really more like a frozen mousse. It came from Jacqueline Kennedy, who served it at Georgetown dinner parties when she was a Senator's wife.

In a small bowl, sprinkle the gelatin over the water. Set aside.

Place the unsweetened chocolate in a small pan and melt over a pan of hot water, stirring until smooth. Remove from the heat, stir in the confectioners' sugar, and mix well.

Heat the milk in a small saucepan over medium-low heat just until a film appears on the surface. Slowly stir the milk into the chocolate mixture. Mix thoroughly. Cook over low heat, stirring constantly, until the mixture almost reaches the boiling point (do not boil).

Remove the pan from the heat and mix in the softened gelatin, the granulated sugar, vanilla, and salt. Pour into a bowl, cover, and refrigerate, for about 45 minutes, until slightly thickened.

Beat the chocolate mixture with a whisk until light and airy. In a large bowl with an electric mixer, beat the cream until it holds its shape. Fold the cream into the chocolate mixture.

Fold a long 6-inch-wide strip of aluminum foil over lengthwise and lightly oil it on one side. Wrap the foil, oiled-side in, around a 1-quart soufflé dish to make a collar standing 2 inches above the top. Spoon the chocolate mixture into the prepared dish. Refrigerate for at least 3 hours. (The soufflé can be prepared ahead, covered, and refrigerated for 1 day.)

Scrape the bittersweet chocolate with a vegetable peeler to form curls. Carefully remove the collar from the soufflé, garnish with the chocolate curls, and serve.

❖LEMON-POPPY SEED SOUFFLÉS

SERVES 6

1 ½ cups milk

¼ cup poppy seeds

Zest of 2 lemons, removed with a vegetable
    peeler, plus slivered zest for garnish

¾ cup superfine sugar

½ cup all-purpose flour

3 large egg yolks

2 tablespoons Grand Marnier

Juice of 1 lemon

¼ teaspoon salt

6 large egg whites at room temperature

Pinch cream of tartar

Confectioners' sugar, for dusting

No dessert produces as exciting a climax to a meal as a soufflé straight from the oven. These individual lemon soufflés, from Etats Unis restaurant, get an extra kick with the addition of poppy seeds.

Preheat the oven to 350°F. Butter six 4x2½-inch ramekins and sprinkle with sugar. Combine the milk, poppy seeds, and lemon zest in the top of a double boiler set over simmering water and heat until small bubbles begin to appear around the edge. Remove from the heat and let stand for 10 minutes. Discard the lemon zest.

Whisk together the superfine sugar, flour, and egg yolks in a bowl. Add to the warm milk mixture and blend thoroughly. Add the Grand Marnier, lemon juice, and salt. Set the mixture back over simmering water and cook, stirring constantly, until slightly thickened and smooth, about 4 minutes. Remove from the heat and let cool.

In a large bowl with an electric mixer, beat the egg whites with the cream of tartar until soft peaks form. Carefully fold the egg whites into the lemon mixture. Divide the mixture among the prepared ramekins. Bake for 25 to 30 minutes. Dust with confectioners' sugar, garnish with lemon zest, and serve immediately.

❖TOASTED ALMOND PARFAIT

SERVES 8

6 ounces whole natural almonds

About ³/₄ cup pure maple syrup

2 pints vanilla ice cream, softened

¹/₄ cup slivered almonds (or sweetened whipped cream), for garnish

This vintage 1970s recipe is simply a combination of crumbled toasted almonds layered with vanilla ice cream. Assemble the dessert in parfait or wine glasses, garnish with slivered almonds, and serve — it couldn't be easier. It can also be made a week ahead and frozen.

Preheat the oven to 400°F. Place 8 parfait or wine glasses in the refrigerator. Spread the whole almonds on a baking sheet and toast in the oven, shaking the pan occasionally, for about 10 minutes, until golden brown. Cool.

Transfer the almonds to a food processor and process until finely ground. Transfer to a small bowl, add ³/₄ cup maple syrup, and stir to make a thin paste. If the mixture seems too thick, add more maple syrup.

Remove the glasses from the refrigerator and spoon a generous amount of the almond paste into the bottoms of each. Cover with a thick layer of ice cream. Repeat the layering once. Cover each glass with plastic wrap and place in the freezer. (The parfaits can be prepared ahead and kept in the freezer for up to 1 week.)

Thirty minutes before serving transfer the parfaits to the refrigerator to soften slightly. Garnish with slivered almonds and serve.

CORDIALS

Although there will always be those who prefer a glass of sparkling water after dinner, there are others who appreciate a dram of a good single-malt scotch or a thimble of grappa. A silver tray, a bevy of tiny glasses, a bottle of Cognac, Armagnac, Framboise, or Poire William, and you're ready to delight your guests.

❖ SCENTED-GERANIUM ICE CREAM

MAKES ABOUT 3 CUPS

5 to 6 scented geranium leaves (rose, lime, or nutmeg), roughly chopped, plus more for garnish

2 teaspoons scented geranium petals (same type as leaves), plus more for garnish

1¼ cups half-and-half

½ cup sugar

4 large egg yolks

1 cup heavy cream

Fresh flowers can be a wonderful enhancement to desserts; rose-scented geraniums make a particularly delightful addition to summer parties. Here the West Street Grill uses it to perfume vanilla ice cream.

Combine the geranium leaves, geranium petals, and half-and-half in a small saucepan over medium heat. Heat until small bubbles begin to appear around the edge. Set aside to cool for 20 minutes.

In a medium stainless steel saucepan, whisk together the sugar and egg yolks until light and frothy. Whisk the egg mixture into the half-and-half mixture, then pour back into the stainless steel pan. Cook over low heat, stirring constantly with a wooden spoon, until the custard is thick enough to coat the back of the spoon. Strain the custard through a fine strainer into a bowl. Set the bowl in a larger bowl filled with ice water and let cool, stirring occasionally.

In a medium bowl, beat the heavy cream until stiff peaks form. Gently fold in the cooled custard. Pour into an ice cream maker and freeze according to the manufacturer's directions. Transfer to a container and place in the freezer overnight to harden.

Scoop the ice cream into small glasses, garnish with geranium petals and leaves, and serve.

❖ ROSEMARY ICE

MAKES ABOUT 3 CUPS

1½ cups water

¾ cup dry white wine

2 tablespoons sugar

2 tablespoons fresh lemon juice

¼ cup anise-flavored aquavit

½ teaspoon minced fresh rosemary

½ teaspoon minced fresh lemon thyme

Salt, to taste

Fresh herbs are also good for giving desserts a lift. This one, for rosemary ice, comes from the West Street Grill, and is a wonderful palate cleanser. It is especially delicious when accompanied by butter cookies after a summer meal.

Combine all the ingredients in a small stainless steel saucepan over medium heat. Bring to a simmer and simmer for 3 minutes. Transfer to a metal bowl, cover, and place in the freezer. Freeze for 30 minutes, then quickly whisk the partly frozen ice. Continue freezing, whisking every 30 minutes, for 1½ to 2½ hours longer, until the mixture has reached the consistency of slush. Allow the ice to freeze hard overnight. With a fork, break the ice into large chunks. Spoon into bowls or goblets and serve immediately.

❖FROZEN WHITE CHOCOLATE MOUSSE

SERVES 8

3 ounces white chocolate, finely chopped

1/2 cup sugar

3 tablespoons water

2 large eggs, separated

1 cup heavy cream, whipped to stiff peaks

2 tablespoons butter at room temperature

Chopped pistachio nuts, for garnish

These snowy little mounds of white chocolate mousse, from cookbook author Emalee Chapman, are unmolded onto a dessert plate and topped with grated white chocolate and pistachios for a simple presentation.

Melt the white chocolate in the top of a double boiler set over simmering water, stirring until smooth. Add the sugar and water and cook for 2 minutes, stirring constantly. Remove from the heat and let cool.

In a medium bowl with an electric mixer, beat the egg yolks until thick and lemon-colored. Add 2 tablespoons of the chocolate mixture and blend well. Slowly blend in the remaining chocolate mixture.

In a small bowl with an electric mixer, beat the egg whites until stiff peaks form. Gently fold the egg whites into the chocolate mixture. Carefully fold in 1 generous cup of the whipped cream. Cover and refrigerate the remaining whipped cream.

Butter eight 2-inch ramekins. Pour the chocolate mixture into the ramekins, cover and place in the freezer for at least 3 hours. (The dessert can be prepared in advance and kept in the freezer for up to 3 days.)

To serve, place a warm damp cloth around each mold for 30 seconds, then run the blade of a metal spatula around the rim of the mold and invert the mousse onto a dessert plate. Garnish each with a dollop of the reserved whipped cream and some pistachios and serve.

❖CHOCOLATE-GLAZED ANGEL FOOD CAKE

SERVES 8 TO 10

Cake:

1½ cups cake flour

1½ cups confectioners' sugar

1 teaspoon cream of tartar

1½ cups egg whites (from about 12 large eggs) at room temperature

¼ cup granulated sugar

1 teaspoon vanilla extract

Berries:

½ cup white wine

½ cup granulated sugar

2 pints fresh berries, such as strawberries, blackberries, or raspberries

2 tablespoons chopped fresh mint leaves

Chocolate glaze:

½ cup heavy cream

¼ cup milk

8 ounces semisweet chocolate, coarsely chopped

2 tablespoons light corn syrup

An American classic since the 1870s, angel food cake is light and low in fat and calories. The addition of a chocolate glaze, and the accompaniment of berries cooked in wine, give it a celebratory feel.

To prepare the cake, preheat the oven to 350°F. Sift together the flour, confectioners' sugar, and cream of tartar into a large bowl. In another large bowl with an electric mixer, beat the egg whites, granulated sugar, and vanilla on medium speed until soft peaks begin to form. With a rubber spatula gently fold the dry ingredients into the egg whites, being careful not to overmix. Do not try to eliminate all of the lumps, or the cake will be heavy.

Pour the batter into an ungreased 9-inch tube pan, preferably with a removable bottom. Bake for about 45 minutes, until the top of the cake is light brown. Invert the pan onto a wire rack to cool.

To prepare the berries, in a saucepan over medium heat, bring the wine and granulated sugar to a simmer, stirring until the sugar dissolves. Simmer for 3 to 4 minutes, until slightly reduced. Add the berries and cook, stirring, for 1 minute. Let cool. Stir in the mint.

To prepare the chocolate glaze, in a small saucepan over low heat, heat the cream and milk until hot, but do not allow to boil. Add the chocolate and stir to melt. Remove from heat and stir in the corn syrup. Cool until the glaze is a thick and creamy consistency. Remove the cake from the pan and transfer to a serving plate. Pour the chocolate glaze over the cake, slice, and serve with the berries on the side.

❖ FROZEN LEMON ROULADE

SERVES 20

1½ to 2 pints vanilla frozen yogurt or
　　vanilla ice milk

2 tablespoons freshly grated lemon zest

½ cup fresh lemon juice

1 teaspoon lemon extract

One 7x12-inch Génoise (recipe follows), rolled
　　as directed

Fruit coulis:

2 cups fresh or thawed frozen strawberries,
　　raspberries, or boysenberries

This lemon roulade — sponge cake wrapped around a lemon cream filling — is one of the deceptively low-calorie, low-fat desserts that has made the Golden Door Spa in California famous.

In a large bowl with an electric mixer, combine the frozen yogurt, lemon zest, lemon juice, and lemon extract and beat until smooth and creamy but still frozen (beating the frozen yogurt aerates the mixture and makes it creamier and less icy).

Unroll the génoise and spread the frozen yogurt mixture over the surface. Roll up like a jelly roll, wrap in plastic, and refreeze.

To prepare the fruit coulis, process the fruit in a blender or food processor until puréed. Strain through a fine-mesh strainer to remove the seeds.

About 10 minutes before serving, remove the roulade from the freezer and thinly slice. Place the slices on individual dessert plates and let soften slightly. Serve with the coulis on the side.

GÉNOISE

5 large eggs

¾ cup sugar

1 teaspoon freshly grated lemon zest

¼ teaspoon freshly grated nutmeg

1 teaspoon vanilla extract

1 cup all-purpose flour

Confectioners' sugar, for sprinkling

Preheat the oven to 350°F. Spray a 7x12-inch jelly-roll pan with nonstick cooking spray and line with parchment paper. In a metal mixing bowl set over a pan of simmering water, whisk together the eggs, sugar, lemon zest, and nutmeg. Whisk continuously until the mixture reaches 120°F (hot to the touch). Remove from the heat and beat until the mixture has tripled in volume and the bowl is cool. Whisk in the vanilla and carefully fold in the flour. Spread the batter into the prepared pan.

Bake the génoise for 12 to 15 minutes, until puffy and lightly browned. Turn the génoise out onto a sheet of parchment paper sprinkled with confectioners' sugar. Peel the parchment paper from the génoise and starting from a long side, roll as you would a jelly roll. (The génoise can be prepared ahead, tightly wrapped, and stored in the freezer for up to 1 week.)

Simply Chic

Fashion designer Bill Blass is famous for creating boldly colored suits and shimmering evening dresses that define urban sophistication. But at his weekend home in the country, calm and simplicity reign. He is forever editing, paring down, and refining his possessions. Even when it comes to color, less is more for the designer. He finds all he needs in his garden, from which he arranges bouquets of flowers to place around the house. The rest of his home and table draw on a more muted palette of brown, sepia, and cream.

His tabletop usually includes an artful arrangement of pears — never flowers — surrounded by classic pieces of antique china, silver candlesticks, and glasses. His meals feature down-home no-frills fare; meatloaf, succotash, and mashed potatoes comprise a favorite entertaining menu. "I don't serve a first course in the country," the designer explains. "It's not necessary if you have a hearty meal and pass it around twice." Perhaps the only extravagance in his straightforward classic schemes is a rich, fruit-based dessert or tea with a selection of seductive cakes. Blass loves them all. This is elegant country fare at its best.

Child's Play at Teatime

You're never too young to learn the delights of afternoon tea, says *House Beautiful* columnist Dee Hardie, whose tea parties are great treats for her grandchildren, their young cousins, and their friends. Every month two cousins — Arthur, five, and Linn, four — come racing into the house calling out, "Tea, please, and lots of honey," and Dee obliges. Her teenage granddaughter Edith helps set the table. For this Easter gathering, a pale yellow cloth shows off an enchanting collection of children's tea party paraphernalia — Beatrix Potter china mixed with miniature tea sets, china rabbits holding place cards, and a centerpiece of stuffed bunnies in fancy dress sitting around on tiny painted chairs.

Once the guests are seated Dee serves hot cross buns, scones, butter pats shaped with a rabbit cookie cutter, and jam. Iced carrot cake and cookies come a bit later. After half an hour — about the limit for tea table manners — it's off to play some games. Sometimes that means rummaging through Dee's closets and dressing up in her clothes. "We try on hats and play with pocketbooks," says Dee, who keeps a trunkful of vintage models handy. On special occasions the children put on a little show, directed by Edith. In the summer it's hide-and-seek in the garden. All in all, it's an invitation to play "grown-up" in the most delightful way.

le tea; and she gave a dose of ...

Peter was not very well during the evening.
His mother put him to bed.

Edith

and made som...
'One table-spo...

PHOTOGRAPHY CREDITS

i	A. Bootz	51c	M. Arnaud	121	O. Gili
ii	R. Felber	52	M. Acevedo	122	A. Bootz
iv	J. Jensen	53	M. Acevedo	123	D. Gallagher
vi	T. McWilliam	55	D. Gallagher	124	M. Acevedo
vii	A. Bootz	56	T. Jeanson	128	O. Gili
viiiA	R. Felber	57	Gentl & Hyers	129a	O. Gili
viiiB	J. Vaughan	59	E. Zeschin	129b	O. Gili
ixA	A. Bootz	60	A. Bootz	130	E. Zeschin
ixB	A. Bootz	61a	A. Bootz	131a	E. Zeschin
xi	V. Pearson	61b	A. Bootz	131b	E. Zeschin
xiii	A. Bootz	62	A. Bootz	132	A. Bootz
xiv	R. Felber	64	A. Bootz	134	J. Vaughan
2	Gentl & Hyers	66	D. Gallagher	136	N. Milne
3	Gentl & Hyers	68	D. Gallagher	137	N. Milne
4	C. Baker	71	D. Gallagher	138	J. Vaughan
6	L. Himmel	73	A. Bootz	140a	E. Zeschin
8	Gentl & Hyers	74	J. Kallina	140b	E. Zeschin
9	Gentl & Hyers	75	A. Bootz	141	E. Zeschin
10	D. Gallagher	76	A. Bootz	142	O. Gili
12	M. Acevedo	77	A. Bootz	143	M. Acevedo
14	Gentl & Hyers	78	M. Acevedo	144	D. Gallagher
16	L. Himmel	79a	A. Bootz	145	O. Gili
17	R. Felber	79b	A. Bootz	147	Gentl & Hyers
18	D. Gallagher	79c	A. Bootz	149	P. Bosch
20	D. Gallagher	80	Gentl & Hyers	150	M. Acevedo
21	A. Bootz	83	T. Eckerle	151	T. Eckerle
22	A. Bootz	84	R. Felber	153	Gentl & Hyers
25	Gentl & Hyers	86	E. Zeschin	154	J. Dirand
26	Gentl & Hyers	88	J. Vaughan	155	V. Pearson
29	A. Bootz	91	A. Bootz	156a	S. Frances
30a	E. Zeschin	95	Gentl & Hyers	156b	D. Vorillon
30b	E. Zeschin	97	A. Bootz	157	M. Acevedo
31	E. Zeschin	98a	A. Garn	158	M. Acevedo
32	J. Vaughan	98b	M. Acevedo	159	Gentl & Hyers
34	P. Bosch	99	M. Acevedo	160	A. Bootz
36	V. Pearson	100	A. Bootz	161	M. Acevedo
38a	O. Gili	101	O. Gili	162	A. Bootz
38b	R. Felber	102	A. Bootz	163	A. Bootz
39a	R. Felber	103	A. Bootz	164	E. Zeschin
39b	A. Bailhache	104	A. Bootz	166	A. Bootz
41	D. Gallagher	105	Gentl & Hyers	167	A. Bootz
42	R. Felber	106	R. Felber	168	A. Bootz
43	Gentl & Hyers	107	C. Baker	170a	M. Acevedo
44	D. Gallagher	110	K. Haavisto	170b	M. Acevedo
45	T. Eckerle	112	Gentl & Hyers	170c	M. Acevedo
46	A. Bootz	116	O. Gili	170d	M. Acevedo
48	A. Bootz	117	D. Gallagher	171	M. Acevedo
51a	L. Himmel	119	M. Acevedo	172	E. Zeschin
51b	A. Bootz	120	D. Gallagher	178	M. Acevedo

RECIPE INDEX

AïOLI
Asparagus with Rosemary Aïoli, 20
ALMONDS
Lemon Almond Pound Cake, 143
Toasted Almond Parfait, 160
Ambrosia, 139
Anchoïade, 5
ANCHOVIES
Anchoïade, 5
Tuscan Bread Salad, 49
Angel Hair Pasta with Caviar, 73
APPLES
Beet and Apple on Endive, 11
Grilled Pork Chops and Apples, 108
Rustic Apple Tart, 144
APRICOTS
Apricot and Cherry Clafouti, 139
Apricot Sauce, 150
Apricot Tart, 145
ASPARAGUS
Asparagus Risotto, 74
Asparagus with Rosemary Aïoli, 20
Lemon Asparagus, 127
Risotto Pesto Primavera, 75
Atlantic Fish Ragout with Saffron
Mayonnaise, 87
Avocado, Pink Grapefruit, and Orange
Salad with Lemon-Pepper
Dressing, 46

Balsamic Vinaigrette, 19
BARLEY
Mushroom-Barley Soup, 37
Basque Chicken, 91
Bay Scallops Sauce Vierge, 21
BEANS
Black Bean Gazpacho, 41
Black-Eyed Pea Salsa, 54
Cassoulet, 109
Escarole and White Bean Soup, 40
Succotash, 122
West Street Grill Bean Salad, 54
White Bean Purée, 4
BEANS, GREEN
Haricots Verts and Water Chestnut
Salad, 49
BEEF
Bill Blass's Meat Loaf, 102
Semolina Gnocchi with Meat Ragu, 72
Stilton Sirloin Burgers, 100
BEER
Pork Roasted in Beer, 107
BEETS
Beet and Apple on Endive, 11

Salad of Endive, Orange, and Beets
with Beet Vinaigrette, 50
Beggars' Purses, 13
Bill Blass's Meat Loaf, 102
BISCUITS
Seafood Pot Pie with Tarragon
Biscuits, 86
Black Bean Gazpacho, 41
Black-Eyed Pea Salsa, 54
Braised Lamb Shanks, 106
Brandade de Morue, 24
BREAD
Chocolate Bread Pudding, 152
Tuscan Bread Salad, 49
BROCCOLI
Risotto Pesto Primavera, 75
BROCCOLI RABE
Penne with Broccoli Rabe and Pine
Nuts, 67
BRUSSELS SPROUTS
Roasted Vegetables, 117
Butternut Consommé, 44

CAKE
Chocolate-Glazed Angel Food
Cake, 164
Génoise, 165
Lemon Almond Pound Cake, 143
Pound Cake with Lemon Glaze, 142
Strawberry Shortcake with Hot
Cream Sauce, 135
CARROTS
Moroccan Spiced Carrots with
Cumin-Honey Vinaigrette, 119
Roasted Vegetables, 117
Root Vegetable Pancakes with Ginger
Dipping Sauce, 12
Cassoulet, 109
Cauliflower with Fresh Herb
Vinaigrette, 118
CAVIAR
Angel Hair Pasta with Caviar, 73
Céleri Rémoulade, 14
CHARD
Swiss Chard Timbales, 126
Charlie Palmer's Honey Tuiles, 3
Charlie Palmer's Parmesan Tuiles, 3
CHEESE
Charlie Palmer's Parmesan Tuiles, 3
Grilled Vegetable Antipasto with
Chèvre, 19
Lemon Ricotta Hotcakes, 142
Shropshire Blue Cheese Souffléed
Puddings, 27

Stilton Sirloin Burgers, 100
Stilton with Roasted Pears, 5
Strawberries with Mascarpone, 135
CHERRIES
Apricot and Cherry Clafouti, 139
Roasted Duck with Warm
Cherries, 97
CHICK PEAS
Black Bean Gazpacho, 41
CHICKEN
Basque Chicken, 91
Chicken Pot Pie, 93
Chicken with Pancetta, Potatoes, and
Black Olives, 90
Curried Breast of Chicken on Rice
Salad, 89
Poached Roulade of Chicken, 92
Roasted Chicken, 90
Thai-Skewered Chicken, 7
CHOCOLATE
Chocolate Bread Pudding, 152
Chocolate-Glazed Angel Food
Cake, 164
Chocolate Pears, 137
Chocolate Soufflés, 153
Chocolate Tart, 151
Cold Chocolate Soufflé, 158
CHOCOLATE, WHITE
Frozen White Chocolate Mousse, 163
Citrus Sauce, 82
CLAFOUTI
Apricot and Cherry Clafouti, 139
CLAMS
Atlantic Fish Ragout with Saffron
Mayonnaise, 87
Clementine, Fennel, and Moroccan Olive
Salad, 52
COD
Atlantic Fish Ragout with Saffron
Mayonnaise, 87
Brandade de Morue, 24
Cold Chocolate Soufflé, 158
Coriander-Cured Salmon, 22
CORN
Fresh Corn Relish, 28
Parsley and Chive Corn Cakes with
Fresh Corn Relish, 28
Succotash, 122
COUSCOUS
Couscous Salad, 55
Lemon Vegetable Couscous, 124
CRAB
Jonah Crab Soup with Winter
Vegetables, 35

Spicy Crab Cakes, 85
Cranberry Oil, 111
Crisp Roasted Salmon with Citrus
    Sauce, 82
CROSTINI
    Crostini with Four Toppings, 4
    Garlic Crostini, 42
Cumberland Sausage Stuffing, 96
Curried Breast of Chicken on Rice
    Salad, 89
Curried Salmon en Papillote, 81

D'Artagnan, 17
DUCK
    Cassoulet, 109
    Roasted Duck with Warm
        Cherries, 97

EGGPLANT
    Eggplant Salad with Almonds, Dates,
        and Mint, 53
    Neapolitan-Style Eggplant, 125
    Roasted Vegetables, 117
ENDIVE
    Beet and Apple on Endive, 11
    Salad of Endive, Orange, and Beets
        with Beet Vinaigrette, 50
Escarole and White Bean Soup, 40
Evelyn Lauder's Potato Salad, 114

FENNEL
    Clementine, Fennel, and Moroccan
        Olive Salad, 52
    Leek and Fennel Soup, 37
FISH see also SEAFOOD
    Atlantic Fish Ragout with Saffron
        Mayonnaise, 87
    Brandade de Morue, 24
    Coriander-Cured Salmon, 22
    Crisp Roasted Salmon with Citrus
        Sauce, 82
    Curried Salmon en Papillote, 81
    Lemon-Scented Fettuccine with
        Smoked Salmon, 69
    New England Seafood Chowder, 84
    Salmon Tartare on Six-Grain Bread, 10
    Seafood Pot Pie with Tarragon
        Biscuits, 86
    Smoked Haddock Chowder, 36
Fresh Corn Relish, 28
Frozen Lemon Roulade, 165
Frozen White Chocolate Mousse, 163
FRUIT
    Ambrosia, 139
    Apricot and Cherry Clafouti, 139

Apricot Tart, 145
Chocolate Pears, 137
Frozen Lemon Roulade, 165
Poached Pears with Brandy and
    Ginger, 136
Rustic Apple Tart, 144
Strawberries with Mascarpone, 135
Strawberry Shortcake with Hot
    Cream Sauce, 135

Garlic-Cilantro Pork Tenderloin, 107
Garlic Crostini, 42
GAZAPACHO
    Black Bean Gazpacho, 41
    Gazpacho, 40
Génoise, 165
GERANIUMS
    Scented-Geranium Ice Cream, 162
Giblet Gravy, 96
GINGER
    James Beard's Pumpkin Pie with
        Candied Ginger, 146
    Poached Pears with Brandy and
        Ginger, 136
GNOCCHI
    Semolina Gnocchi with Meat Ragu, 72
GRAPEFRUIT
    Avocado, Pink Grapefruit, and
        Orange Salad with Lemon-Pepper
        Dressing, 46
GRAVY
    Giblet Gravy, 96
Greek Village Salad, 46
Green Chile Country-Style Potatoes, 112
GREENS
    Escarole and White Bean Soup, 40
    Mixed Winter Greens with Bacon, 121
    Swiss Chard Timbales, 126
Grilled Pork Chops and Apples, 108
Grilled Shrimp and Vegetables, 83
Grilled Vegetable Antipasto with Chèvre,
    19
Grits Soufflé, 115

HADDOCK
    Smoked Haddock Chowder, 36
Haricots Verts and Water Chestnut
    Salad, 49
Herbed Veal Bundles, 103
Holiday Martini, 17
HOTCAKES
    Lemon Ricotta Hotcakes, 142

ICE

Rosemary Ice, 162
ICE CREAM
    Scented-Geranium Ice Cream, 162
    Toasted Almond Parfait, 160

James Beard's Onion Sandwiches, 9
James Beard's Pumpkin Pie with Candied
    Ginger, 146
Jimtown Seafood Cocktail, 23
Jonah Crab Soup with Winter
    Vegetables, 35

LAMB
    Braised Lamb Shanks, 106
    Cassoulet, 109
    Lamb Stew with New Potatoes, 104
    Shepherd's Pie, 105
Le Perroquet, 17
LEEK
    Leek and Fennel Soup, 37
    Roasted Leeks, 118
    Roasted Vegetables, 117
LEMONS
    Frozen Lemon Roulade, 165
    Lemon Almond Pound Cake, 143
    Lemon Asparagus, 127
    Lemon Oil, 127
    Lemon-Poppy Seed Soufflés, 159
    Lemon Ricotta Hotcakes, 142
    Lemon-Scented Fettuccine with
        Smoked Salmon, 69
    Lemon Vegetable Couscous, 124
    Pound Cake with Lemon Glaze, 142
    Preserved Lemons, 119
LENTILS
    Lentil Soup with Sage Crème
        Fraîche, 43
    Old-Fashioned Lentil Salad, 56
Linguine with Olive Oil and Chives, 67
LOBSTER
    Atlantic Fish Ragout with Saffron
        Mayonnaise, 87
    Beggars' Purses, 13
    New England Seafood Chowder, 84

Maple Walnut Tart, 148
Mashed Potatoes with Herbs, 112
MEAT
    Bill Blass's Meat Loaf, 102
    Cassoulet, 109
    Pasta Shells with Wild Mushroom
        Meat Ragu, 70
    Seared Three-Pepper Venison Chops
        with Three-Lily Jam, 110

Semolina Gnocchi with Meat Ragu, 72
Shepherd's Pie, 105
Stilton Sirloin Burgers, 100
Mixed Winter Greens with Bacon, 121
Moroccan Spiced Carrots with Cumin-
Honey Vinaigrette, 119
MOUSSE
Frozen White Chocolate Mousse, 163
MUSHROOMS
Mushroom-Barley Soup, 37
Pasta Shells with Wild Mushroom
Meat Ragu, 70
Roasted Shiitake Mushrooms, 5
Sautéed Salsify with Bacon,
Mushrooms, and Pearl Onions, 120
Wild Rice with Porcini Duxelles, 116
MUSSELS
Atlantic Fish Ragout with Saffron
Mayonnaise, 87
Mussels in White Wine, 23

Neapolitan-Style Eggplant, 125
New England Seafood Chowder, 84
November Pudding, 150

Old-Fashioned Lentil Salad, 56
OLIVES
Chicken with Pancetta, Potatoes, and
Black Olives, 90
Clementine, Fennel, and Moroccan
Olive Salad, 52
Greek Village Salad, 46
Spaghetti with Fresh Tomato Sauce
and Olives, 69
ONIONS
James Beard's Onion Sandwiches, 9
Sautéed Salsify with Bacon,
Mushrooms, and Pearl Onions, 120
Shallots in Red Wine, 123
Three-Lily Jam, 111
Tomato, Red Onion, and Mint Salad, 50
ORANGES
Ambrosia, 139
Avocado, Pink Grapefruit, and Orange
Salad with Lemon-Pepper
Dressing, 46
Clementine, Fennel, and Moroccan
Olive Salad, 52
Salad of Endive, Orange, and Beets
with Beet Vinaigrette, 50
Organic Herb Salad with Balsamic
Vinaigrette, 48
OYSTERS
Roast Quail and Corn-Fried Oyster
Cobb Salad, 58

PANCAKES
Lemon Ricotta Hotcakes, 142
Root Vegetable Pancakes with Ginger
Dipping Sauce, 12
PANCETTA
Chicken with Pancetta, Potatoes, and
Black Olives, 90
PARFAIT
Toasted Almond Parfait, 160
Parsley and Chive Corn Cakes with
Fresh Corn Relish, 28
PARSNIPS
Parsnip Gratin, 123
Root Vegetable Pancakes with Ginger
Dipping Sauce, 12
Passion Fruit Soup, 45
PASTA
Angel Hair Pasta with Caviar, 73
Lemon-Scented Fettuccine with
Smoked Salmon, 69
Linguine with Olive Oil and Chives, 67
Pasta Shells with Wild Mushroom
Meat Ragu, 70
Penne with Broccoli Rabe and Pine
Nuts, 67
Semolina Gnocchi with Meat Ragu, 72
Spaghetti with Fresh Tomato Sauce
and Olives, 69
PEARS
Chocolate Pears, 137
Poached Pears with Brandy and
Ginger, 136
Stilton with Roasted Pears, 5
PECANS
Ambrosia, 139
Pecan Pie, 146
Penne with Broccoli Rabe and Pine
Nuts, 67
PEPPERS
Basque Chicken, 91
Black Bean Gazpacho, 41
Gazpacho, 40
Grilled Vegetable Antipasto with
Chèvre, 19
Lemon Vegetable Couscous, 124
Roasted Peppers Stuffed with
Walnuts, 122
Roasted Red and Yellow Peppers, 121
Roasted Red Pepper Soup, 42
Roasted Vegetables, 117
PIE see also TARTS
James Beard's Pumpkin Pie with
Candied Ginger, 146
Pecan Pie, 146
Poached Pears with Brandy and Ginger,
136

Poached Roulade of Chicken, 92
PORK
Bill Blass's Meat Loaf, 102
Garlic-Cilantro Pork Tenderloin, 107
Grilled Pork Chops and Apples, 108
Pork Roasted in Beer, 107
Semolina Gnocchi with Meat Ragu, 72
POTATOES
Brandade de Morue, 24
Chicken with Pancetta, Potatoes, and
Black Olives, 90
Evelyn Lauder's Potato Salad, 114
Green Chile Country-Style
Potatoes, 112
Lamb Stew with New Potatoes, 104
Mashed Potatoes with Herbs, 112
Shepherd's Pie, 105
POTATOES, SWEET
Root Vegetable Pancakes with Ginger
Dipping Sauce, 12
Sweet Potato Purée, 114
POT PIE
Seafood Pot Pie with Tarragon
Biscuits, 86
Chicken Pot Pie, 93
POUND CAKE
Lemon Almond Pound Cake, 143
Pound Cake with Lemon Glaze, 142
Preserved Lemons, 119
PUDDING
November Pudding, 150
PUMPKIN
James Beard's Pumpkin Pie with
Candied Ginger, 146

QUAIL
Roast Quail and Corn-Fried Oyster
Cobb Salad, 58

RADICCHIO
Sea Scallop Ceviche in Radicchio, 11
RICE
Curried Breast of Chicken on Rice
Salad, 89
Saffron Rice, 115
Wild Rice with Porcini Duxelles, 116
RISOTTO
Asparagus Risotto, 74
Risotto Pesto Primavera, 75
Roast Quail and Corn-Fried Oyster
Cobb Salad, 58
Roasted Chicken, 90
Roasted Duck with Warm Cherries, 97
Roasted Leeks, 118
Roasted Peppers Stuffed with
Walnuts, 122

Roasted Red and Yellow Peppers, 121
Roasted Red Pepper Soup, 42
Roasted Shiitake Mushrooms, 5
Roasted Turkey with Chipolatas, 94
Roasted Vegetables, 117
Root Vegetable Pancakes with Ginger
Dipping Sauce, 12
Rosemary Ice, 162
Rustic Apple Tart, 144

Saffron Rice, 115
Salad of Endive, Orange, and Beets with
Beet Vinaigrette, 50
SALMON
Coriander-Cured Salmon, 22
Crisp Roasted Salmon with Citrus
Sauce, 82
Curried Salmon en Papillote, 81
Salmon Tartare on Six-Grain Bread, 10
SALSA
Black-Eyed Pea Salsa, 54
SALSIFY
Sautéed Salsify with Bacon,
Mushrooms, and Pearl Onions, 120
SAUSAGE
Cassoulet, 109
Cumberland Sausage Stuffing, 96
Roasted Turkey with Chipolatas, 94
Sautéed Salsify with Bacon, Mushrooms,
and Pearl Onions, 120
SCALLOPS
Bay Scallops Sauce Vierge, 21
Jimtown Seafood Cocktail, 23
New England Seafood Chowder, 84
Sea Scallop Ceviche in Radicchio, 11
Scented-Geranium Ice Cream, 162
SEAFOOD see also FISH
Atlantic Fish Ragout with Saffron
Mayonnaise, 87
Bay Scallops Sauce Vierge, 21
Grilled Shrimp and Vegetables, 83
Jimtown Seafood Cocktail, 23
Jonah Crab Soup with Winter
Vegetables, 35
Mussels in White Wine, 23
New England Seafood Chowder, 84
Roast Quail and Corn-Fried Oyster
Cobb Salad, 58
Sea Scallop Ceviche in Radicchio, 11
Seafood Pot Pie with Tarragon
Biscuits, 86
Spicy Crab Cakes, 85
Seared Three-Pepper Venison Chops with
Three-Lily Jam, 110
Semolina Gnocchi with Meat Ragu, 72
Shallots in Red Wine, 123

Shepherd's Pie, 105
SHORTCAKE
Strawberry Shortcake with Hot
Cream Sauce, 135
SHRIMP
Atlantic Fish Ragout with Saffron
Mayonnaise, 87
Grilled Shrimp and Vegetables, 83
Jimtown Seafood Cocktail, 23
New England Seafood Chowder, 84
Seafood Pot Pie with Tarragon
Biscuits, 86
Shropshire Blue Cheese Souffléed
Puddings, 27
Slow-Roasted Tomatoes, 20
Smoked Haddock Chowder, 36
SNAPPER, RED
Seafood Pot Pie with Tarragon
Biscuits, 86
SOUFFLÉS
Chocolate Soufflés, 153
Cold Chocolate Soufflé, 158
Grits Soufflé, 115
Lemon-Poppy Seed Soufflés, 159
Shropshire Blue Cheese Souffléed
Puddings, 27
Spaghetti with Fresh Tomato Sauce and
Olives, 69
Spicy Crab Cakes, 85
Spinach Purée in Phyllo, 124
SQUASH
Butternut Consommé, 44
Grilled Vegetable Antipasto with
Chèvre, 19
Lemon Vegetable Couscous, 124
Risotto Pesto Primavera, 75
Stuffed Summer Squash, 127
Stilton Sirloin Burgers, 100
Stilton with Roasted Pears, 5
STRAWBERRIES
Strawberries with Mascarpone, 135
Strawberry Shortcake with Hot
Cream Sauce, 135
Stuffed Summer Squash, 127
Succotash, 122
Summer Salad, 48
SWEET POTATOES
Root Vegetable Pancakes with Ginger
Dipping Sauce, 12
Sweet Potato Purée, 114
Swiss Chard Timbales, 126

TARTS see also PIES
Apricot Tart, 145
Chocolate Tart, 151
Maple Walnut Tart, 148

Rustic Apple Tart, 144
Thai-Skewered Chicken, 7
Three-Lily Jam, 111
Toasted Almond Parfait, 160
TOMATOES
Black Bean Gazpacho, 41
Gazpacho, 40
Greek Village Salad, 46
Jimtown Seafood Cocktail, 23
Slow-Roasted Tomatoes, 20
Spaghetti with Fresh Tomato Sauce
and Olives, 69
Tomato, Red Onion, and Mint Salad, 50
Tuscan Bread Salad, 49
TRUFFLES
Beggars' Purses, 13
TUNA
Anchoïade, 5
TUILES
Charlie Palmer's Honey Tuiles, 3
Charlie Palmer's Parmesan Tuiles, 3
TURKEY
Roasted Turkey with Chipolatas, 94
Tuscan Bread Salad, 49

VEAL
Bill Blass's Meat Loaf, 102
Herbed Veal Bundles, 103
Pasta Shells with Wild Mushroom
Meat Ragu, 70
VENSION
Seared Three-Pepper Venison Chops
with Three-Lily Jam, 110

WALNUTS
Maple Walnut Tart, 148
WATER CHESTNUTS
Haricots Verts and Water Chestnut
Salad, 49
West Street Grill Bean Salad, 54
White Bean Purée, 4
Wild Rice with Porcini Duxelles, 116